HORATIO. Well, my lord;
If he steal aught the whilst this play is playing
and 'scape detecting, I will pay the theft.

THE HIDDEN SHAKESPEARE

A Study of the Poet's Undercover Activity in the Theatre

Madalyn of Santa Fe

THOMAS H. JAMESON, a tutor at St. John's College in Santa Fe, New Mexico, is well known for his critical work in the Renaissance and Elizabethan fields.

THE HIDDEN SHAKESPEARE

A Study of the Poet's Undercover Activity in the Theatre

THOMAS JAMESON

Funk & Wagnalls New York

First Printing

Library of Congress Catalog Card Number 67-28569
Published by Funk & Wagnalls, A Division of
Reader's Digest Books, Inc.
Printed in the United States of America

TO ANN

"A lass unparallel'd"

CONTENTS

Foreword ix

1 *Henry V: When Art Was Tongue-tied by Authority* 3

2 *Henry IV: The Debt Prince Hal Never Promised* 75

3 *Some Undercover Literary Skirmishing* 132

Appendix 162

Index 165

FOREWORD

The writer on Shakespeare has not made it easy for the lay reader. On the one hand, he has assured him that Shakespeare wrote for all time, on the other that he cannot be properly understood without considerable knowledge of the Renaissance and Tudor times in which he wrote—which unfortunately now include a large element of nostalgia for the Middle Ages. In this book, such a reader will find but one demand made upon him—beside that of having read the six plays under discussion—that he respond to the playwright with his most elementary and familiar store of human feelings. Perhaps unrealistically, it is hoped also that he will have read, recently enough to recall them in some detail, the following plays: *Richard II,* the two parts of *Henry IV, Henry V, A Midsummer-Night's Dream,* and *The Winter's Tale.* It will do no harm if, in addition, he knows his *King Lear* and *As You Like It.*

For the student of Shakespeare, I offer certain well-founded surmises on the subject of what, for want of another name, I shall have to call Shakespeare's "politics." Not since John Danby made his lone scouting expedition in 1949 has anything quite approaching justice, book-length justice, been done to the subject. There have been short essays and studies that have made a good start, but I fancy that the majority is as persuaded as ever that the playwright was a political conservative—or, along with Alfred Harbage, that "he had no politics."

The general reader, however, may be quite unaware of such issues. For him there is the famous inscrutability. "We shall never know" has become an article of faith so strong that the mildest conjecture about what lies behind the comic or the tragic mask may seem to him a kind of betrayal of the master. A disservice results for both parties: the reader's normal human responses are inhibited (for we set no great stock by inscrutability in our daily lives), and Shakespeare fails to convey what he might have wished to convey. What, for example is inscrutable in the following, Sonnet 125?

Were 't aught to me I bore the canopy,
With my extern the outward honouring,
Or laid great bases for eternity,
Which prove more short than waste or ruining?
Have I not seen dwellers on form and favour
Lose all and more by paying too much rent,
For compound sweet foregoing simple savour
Pitiful thrivers, in their gazing spent?
No; let me be obsequious in thy heart,
And take thou my oblation, poor but free,
Which is not mix'd with seconds, knows no art,
But mutual render, only me for thee.

Hence, thou suborn'd informer! a true soul
When most impeach'd stands least in thy control.*

Indeed, I can think of no better preface for a book bearing the subtitle, "Shakespeare's Undercover Activities."

The persons to whom I should like to pay a debt of thanks accrued over the years while the book was waiting for a publisher are Peter Alexander, William Barrett, Richard Harrier, Fred Johnson, and especially Mack Rosenthal and Emile Capouya, who remembered a no longer so young manuscript.

Thomas H. Jameson

Santa Fe, New Mexico

* All quotations from the plays and the sonnets are from *The Oxford Standard Authors* edition: *Shakespeare, Complete Works,* ed. W. J. Craig (London, Oxford University Press, 1943).

THE HIDDEN SHAKESPEARE

A Study of the Poet's Undercover Activity in the Theatre

1 HENRY V
When Art Was Tongue-tied by Authority

It is likely that *The Life of King Henry the Fifth* was one of the plays written by Shakespeare during a low period in his life, the year 1599. Things were much out of joint in the years immediately preceding Elizabeth's death—court favorites fallen out of grace, an unpopular Irish war, open scheming for the succession, censorship of books and play productions. It is no great wonder that none of the plays Shakespeare produced in those years (exclusive of comedies) contain what we are prone to think of as "whole" heroes or protagonists.

The least whole of the lot by far is Harry Monmouth from *Henry V*. Coming to this play fresh from reading the preceding Histories one may be forgiven for asking, "What on earth has happened to Prince Hal?" Who is this excessively passionate yet pious man who sprang unheralded out of the Boar's Head Tavern in Eastcheap to become the conqueror of France?

> . . . and the elements
> So mix'd in him that Nature might stand up
> And say to all the world, 'This was a man!'

Any heroic past calls for such heroes, but the lines here quoted no more suit Harry Monmouth than they did Brutus, of whom they were spoken in *Julius Caesar*, produced in the same year, 1599. The huzzas, the guffaws, the spine-tingling, throat-catching speeches that accompany Monmouth to France do honor to a character about as *un*mix'd as can be found outside broadsides and cartoons. Critical judgments of the play vary accordingly. There are those who claim Harry as a paragon of Nature, others who write as if they could not stomach his company. Perhaps Shakespeare intended this confusion.

It is remarkable that when every nook and cranny of Shakespeare's life is ransacked for evidence of what sort of man he was, how he came to be so educated, what his attitude toward his craft was, what he felt to be his various responsibilities, no one has appeared but mildly interested—to judge from all the evidence I have read—in speculating about his feelings concerning censorship. How can such a thing be? Judging by our own mid-twentieth-century concern for the subject, censorship should have been the dominant interest in his professional life in the years when fellow Londoners were being exiled, maimed, tortured, and imprisoned. His latest history play, and the subject of this chapter, capped a series of plays all of which in one way or another lie under suspicion of having been tampered with by official censors. *Henry V* was composed in a veritable climate of censorship. In short, to William Shakespeare the banning of books, the deleting of passages from play-copy, the closing of theatres were anything but matters of gossip and hearsay.

How does a loyal subject feel who is subjected to such inconvenience in his professional life, or how should he feel? Should he fight back, play safe, or pretend that it is of no consequence to him, he at least being one who is well intentioned? It all depends on the writer. Take Shakespeare. The one scholar, and an influential one, who has concerned himself at length with Shakespeare's possible involvement with censors leaves us to draw the astonishing conclusion that Shakespeare may have sanctioned the intrusion and been grateful for it. Calling attention, some thirty-five years ago, to the quantity of explosive matter contained in Part II of *Henry IV,* instead of posing the obvious question—how in the world did it ever get into the play in the first place?—he published a companion essay protesting Shakespeare's total, consistent, and lifelong orthodoxy. It is a remarkable performance.[1] It seems, however, to have suited the taste of our times, for it in itself has become orthodoxy. It was but a few years ago that one of our eminent Shakespearean scholars wrote an opinion of Shakespeare's conservatism that included approval of such things as the cold-blooded massacre of political dissidents.

What image of Shakespeare, the writer, is being preserved here? The image of a mild man? A timorous one? Or of one who was simply fortunate enough to live unscathed by contemporary scandals and oppressions—and, hence, could afford to be "above them"? But he *was* scathed. His plays show it. Let us reread a certain scene from *2 Henry IV,* not on this occasion to show what little difference the deletions of a niggling censor make on the work of a master, but how great! [2]

The most prominent "rebels" in *2 Henry IV* are a group of men whose chief and most pressing complaint—if the censor would but leave the play alone—is that they are not trusted. They cannot gain the ear of their king even to present their grievances. Granted that this is not the strongest reason for leading an army into the field, let us overlook the impropriety for the moment and hear the Archbishop confiding in his rebel followers. He is answering the pessimistic objections of his confederate Mowbray in a conference that followed their meeting with representatives of the King's forces.

> No, no, my lord. Note this; the King is weary
> Of dainty and such picking grievances:
> For he hath found to end one doubt by death
> Revives two greater in the heirs of life;
> And therefore will he wipe his tables clean,
> And keep no tell-tale to his memory
> That may repeat and history his loss
> To new remembrance; for full well he knows
> He cannot so precisely weed this land
> As his misdoubts present occasion:
> His foes are so enrooted with his friends

That, plucking to unfix an enemy,
He doth unfasten so and shake a friend.
So that this land, like an offensive wife,
That hath enrag'd him on to offer strokes,
As he is striking, holds his infant up
And hangs resolv'd correction in the arm
That was uprear'd to execution.

(IV, i, 197–214)

A peculiarly domestic image we have here, of a wife venturing to remind an angry husband of their shared interests, but no more so than the whole of this scene, that of the meeting of the Archbishop and his confederates with the loyal leaders:

I take not on me here as a physician,
Nor do I as an enemy to peace
Troop in the throngs of military men;
But rather show a while like fearful war,
To diet rank minds sick of happiness
And purge the obstructions which begin to stop
Our very veins of life. . . .

(*Ibid.*, 60–66)

There are thiry-five lines in all of the Archbishop's intended mollification, only ten of which ever reached print in Shakespeare's lifetime. I transcribe the ten, placing asterisks to show where the deletion occurs. It is a feeble exoneration, and feeble it will appear in print:

> Wherefore do I this? so the question stands.
> Briefly to this end: we are all diseas'd;*
> * The dangers of the days but newly gone,—
> Whose memory is written on the earth
> With yet appearing blood,—and the examples
> Of every minute's instance, present now,
> Have put us in these ill-beseeming arms;
> Not to break peace, or any branch of it,
> But to establish here a peace indeed,
> Concurring both in name and quality.
> (*Ibid.*, 53–87)

Let us summarize. What an audience may have heard at the Curtain theatre and what some of them could read for themselves in print at a later date are entirely different things. Gone in the quarto was any reference to Richard, for it was said that Elizabeth could not tolerate any reference to her "weak" predecessor; gone the echo of his joke, in the play already written about him, to his disgruntled nobles, that he did not fancy himself enough of a physician to cure a land ("Our doctors say this is no month to bleed," *Richard II,* I, i, 157); gone the interesting allusion to minds sick of happiness; above all—for this is the crux of the matter—gone the complaints of the insurgents of being denied access to the King's person. Ten lines alone remain, lines sufficient to establish the usual excuse of rebels that they are in the field not to disturb peace but to secure it. The answer delivered by the leader of the loyal forces, "Whenever yet was your appeal denied?"—though hardly an intelligible rebuttal in the absence of any reference to such appeals—was allowed by the censor to stand.

Obviously, none of this can be said to prove crown censorship. Over and above the routine need of actors to shorten their script for production purposes, there is always the alternate possibility of self-censorship,[3] steps taken by their officers to preclude any unnecessary trouble if and when they released a play to be set up in print, the rule being that what escapes notice on the boards may well not do so in print. (I shall return to the suggestion in connection with a disputed passage in *Richard II.*) From rehearsal to compositor's "copy," we are at liberty to imagine a succession of small acts of censorship that we can hardly expect to know anything about. At least, in the present instance, the reader is in possession of all the facts. He knows as much as anyone is likely to know. He will have to base his surmises on the kind of cutting he believes is involved. Cutting that removes possibly objectionable matter, while remaining faithful to the general drift of the text, is different entirely from that which neuters, conceals, or actually perverts its thoughts. The latter are rightly to be considered mutilation. The deletion of the long abdication scene in the first quartos of *Richard II*, for example, provides small ground for positing official censorship. The play required the crown to change hands at some point, and the possibly objectionable feature of the scene—that the restraint of Bolingbroke is made to appear almost magnanimous by contrast with the histrionics of Richard—seems a thing more likely to catch the literary eye than the bureaucratic. The possibility is worth entertaining that the deletion represents voluntary censorship and that it was the failure of officialdom to give proper credit to just such gestures of cooperation that in turn caused a playwright to reexamine his obligations as a wearer of the household livery. "Have I not seen dwellers on form and favour/Lose all and more by paying too much rent?"

In the remaining scenes devoted to the rebels in the interval before their defeat, the Archbishop is allowed another dozen lines of explanation to Prince John himself, very son of "God's substitute," as the latter appropriately refers to his father. If now there is no answer forthcoming to the rebel complaint:

. . . I sent your Grace
The parcels and particulars of our grief,—
The which hath been with scorn shov'd from the court,—
(IV, ii, 35–37)

it is because Shakespeare wrote none. The point he had been making was sufficiently clear, or would have been with the aid of the excised lines. Unhappily, it is just as clear without them—I mean, from the point of view of the crown. The orthodoxy which so many believe Shakespeare to typify may safely rest its case. Like the hostile witness it is shown to be, rebellion is seen largely through crown speeches that dwell on the singularity of an Archbishop's appearance on the field of Mars in armor—in the words of Westmoreland:

Turning your books to greaves, your ink to blood,
Your pens to lances, and your tongue divine
To a loud trumpet and a point of war?
(*Ibid.*, 50–52)

Or, as John of Lancaster will have it:

Turning the word to sword and life to death.
(IV, ii, 10)

Soon enough will John, brother of the Prince of Wales, demonstrate the better use he can find for sacred "Word" in everyday diplomacy. It is a use that appears to have earned him or his like no discredit in Tudor times[4] and unfortunately has not always earned it for him in our own—at least in literary circles.

We now have our groundwork for examining, both in detail and in pervasive tone, the history play next on the boards, *Henry V*. The question remains as before: What might be the feelings and response of an author who has found himself mistaken in an assumption that his sovereign, or the people who represent her in the machinery of government, are weary of "dainty and such picking grievances" and can be mollified by proofs of the common interest held up before them?

Shakespeare's predicament as a writer of popular history plays about his country's unhappy past has been described by no one as well as by Professor Tillyard. With *Henry V*, the time had come, he wrote,[5] to demonstrate to the world at large the glorious results of English unity; yet the means whereby that unity had been achieved were not of a kind to be of much interest to the rest of the world. Not to write a *Henry V* after the other plays would, he wrote, be in the nature of a "scandal," yet at the same time Tudor morality was an article clearly "not for export." In short—though Tillyard does not say this—*Henry V* may very well have been in its way as much of a command performance as *The*

Merry Wives of Windsor is traditionally supposed to have been. What sort of command performance is it that can find no middle ground between, on the one hand, the legitimate splendors of Choruses and a Crispin speech and, on the other, all the near-comic business of throat-cutting and virgin-threatening? Surely, there was no need for the playwright to abandon the safe ground of a rousing play in the mode of *The Famous Victories of Henry the Fifth* or of Michael Drayton's ballad of Agincourt for a bloodthirsty jingoism that could conceivably have offended thinking persons then as much as it does now. Some of his audience, too, would have known that this jingoism was not inherited from any of their author's sources, least of all from Raphael Holinshed, his chief source.

The answer to the puzzle of *Henry V* is, I believe, travesty—travesty strictly defined as disguise or change of garb. It is travesty that is responsible for the mixture of private pacificism and institutional belligerence that so characterizes the play. In resorting to it, Shakespeare did no more than nearly all the wits and journeymen of his day who found themselves with something unpalatable or peculiarly private to say. Assumed heartiness, or the opposite—assumed deference—elaborate pretenses of punctilious scholarship, burlesqued roles, mock attitudes of endless variety, these were the stock-in-trade of the self-conscious writer living in an age of such expected conformity. With his social role far from clarified in any case, and the more so if he wrote for a popular audience, he had good reason to think of himself as politically suspect. I am aware that a volume of statistics should accompany the suggestion, but I hazard the thought nevertheless that to writers of this stamp, circumvention of authority must have appeared part of the business of being an author—the adoption of a pose constituting a sort of insurance. There is a risk of oversimplifying matters. I am well aware that there were other authorities, too, to challenge the self-made author or the unattached one. There were university, Church, antiquity, the full weight of the Middle Ages; and, of course, there is an explanation that cuts across all others, the particular self-consciousness of awakening nationhood.

Shakespeare eternally speaks for the individual; his mightiest political line is his "mutual render, only me for thee." That the experience of writing *Henry V*, and perhaps *2 Henry IV*, was in some manner a disquieting one for him I take to be suggested by the fact that of all his plays these two alone contain statements that it is generally thought represent the author speaking out in his own person. Both take the form of epilogues, and both are apologies. Here are the opening lines of the epilogue of *Henry V*:

> Thus far, with rough and all-unable pen,
> Our bending author hath pursu'd the story;

In little room confining mighty men,
Mangling by starts the full course of their glory.

The "bending" author of these lines is not disposed to give himself credit for five magnificent Choruses, supplying more epic grandeur to his theme than could any quantity of drums, culverins, and marching men. If there is a fatal mangling, it can only superficially be laid to the episodic nature of the whole. The fault lies deeper. As we read in Sonnet 124, it is well for one's nearest and dearest work to be "builded far from accident," where:

It suffers not in smiling pomp, nor falls
Under the blow of thralled discontent,
Whereto the inviting time our fashion calls:
It fears not policy, that heretic,
Which works on leases of short-number'd hours . . .

Like *Merry Wives, Henry V* is a child of state, bearing too clearly the marks of improvisation. It is not the division into five sweeping episodes that is at fault but the general untidiness of those episodes. There is no imaginative overview—except as supplied by the Choruses. Perhaps it deserves the title "Fortune's bastard," though a little more grandly than *Merry Wives.*

Preliminaries past, we are to see how Shakespeare set about, and set about deliberately, in his last chronicle "killing" the thing he loved, burying under a grotesque disguise the vision that had been taking shape of an ideal monarch, bold, warm, humorous and, withal, wise. What the feelings were that accompanied this profanation, whether they were anger, or pique, sorrow, or mocking compliance each will decide for himself.[6] "Sardonic" certainly suits the mood that sees fit to have Harry Monmouth exonerated by a comic Welshman for "killing" Falstaff when a playwright was already doing—or had done—as much under royal injunction. I am referring once again to the weary farce *Merry Wives* and to the tradition that it was completed in fourteen days at the queen's bequest, "to show Falstaff in Love." Be that as it may, a far greater crime was the killing of Prince Hal by turning him into Harry Monmouth.

In the scene alluded to, Fluellan is speaking of his king, but he might as well have been speaking of Elizabeth, equally proud of her Welsh descent and of her great forbear. "Alexander the Pig" may indeed have killed "his pest friend Cleitus" "in his rages, and his furies, and his wraths, and his cholers, and his moods, and his displeasures, and his indignations, and also being a little intoxicates in his prains." But the contemporary of Shakespeare might ask were Elizabeth and her ministers in any better or sounder mind when they . . . But hail to "the leek upon St. Tavy's Day!" As Fluellan says, "there is figures in all things," and the Tudor habit of beheading, banishing, and imprisoning may have an ancient lineage. We who have so often seen Shakespeare savoring his fondness for Plutarch may not have noticed that on this occasion he was also making a commentary on killing. We shall return to this passage further on.

The capacity for self-immolation varies with individuals, though we rather expect that our greatest writers will discharge it through their fictional creations in some more constructive way than driving them mad or killing them off. On this occasion I do not propose to sit in judgment.

> . . . on my frailties why are frailer spies,
> Which in their wills count bad what I think good?
> (Sonnet 121)

I believe that Shakespeare was well aware of the propensity—not counting myself among those who hold that no part of any sonnet may be considered autobiographical. Seeing him sacrifice his Hal in a bumpkin love scene with a French princess, I suggest that we ruefully write it down as a kind of testimony, perhaps the strongest kind of testimony, to the strength of an unrealized ideal. Whatever he did, he chose to do because that was the way he was. The times favored such behavioral extremes, and he had the provocation. We shall next examine in greater detail the extent of the provocation.

2

The time has passed, I believe, when anyone can believe *Henry V* to be a blatantly pro-war play, but neither on the other side does it deserve to be considered an antiwar play. Self-sacrifice and daring such as are called forth in times of war and are depicted in war literature combine to make a pathos that no humanist, however pacific himself, will lightly barter away. William Wordsworth confessed to tears and exaltation at the reading of an account of a sea battle, and I should expect like feelings occasionally to surprise the man who wrote Othello's stirring farewell to the field of honor. Wordsworth, on the other hand, could never have written the lines, "Now set the teeth and stretch the nostrils wide,/Hold hard the breath," best quoted, as I have seen it quoted, in the context of an American sports column. Clearly Shakespeare was skeptical of at least some of the reputed values of war. But does it then follow that he swallowed whole the antiwar propaganda we are told was current in his day and that supposedly he "echoed" in certain of his plays? The following passage is from *Euphues*:

> This is the only miracle that virginity ever wrought: for a little island, environed round about with wars, to stand in

peace; for the walls of France to burn, and the houses of England to freeze; for all other nations either with civil sword to be divided or with foreign foes to be invaded, and that country neither to be molested with broils in their own bosoms nor threatened with blasts of other borderers but always, though not laughing, yet looking through an emerald at others' jars.

This peace hath the Lord continued with great and unspeakable goodness among his chosen people of England. How much is that nation bound to such a prince, by whom they enjoy all benefits of peace; having their barns full when others famish, their coffers stuffed with gold when others have no silver; their wives without danger when others are defamed, their daughters chaste when others are deflowered, their houses furnished when others are fired, where they have all things for superfluity, others nothing to sustain their need. This peace hath God given for her virtues pity moderation virginity; which peace the same God of peace continue for his name's sake.[7]

It would take a brave person indeed to pen such lines today. The smugness, the assumption that it is one's own "restraint" that guarantees peace, the veiled invitation to provocation (to "start something"), have all gone out of fashion across the channel from

France—though I have reason to suspect Englishmen enjoy with their American brothers the exquisite brutalities of the so-called adult Western of recent popularity. Violence is eventually driven underground, and it is for the individual to show by his behavior whether the pacifism he owns to is the genuine or the spurious article. I see no profit in associating Shakespeare with the latter. He was middle-class himself and probably alive to the burgeoning middle-class psyche as it worked itself out in the bear pit and in swaggering encounters with Spanish and Irish soldiery; I for one would like to think that he found such aspects of it repugnant, much as he would if he were alive today.

Although *Henry V* is a military play, written when England was on a military footing, a short review of events may disincline us from attempting to associate him with either doctrinaire view then current, whether that of pacificism or that of militarism. If England was technically at peace, it was peace bought at the price of peace of mind. By 1600 Englishmen were well used to worries and scares over a Spanish invasion (another Armada was reported on its way in this very summer of 1599). For years their ears had been fed with rumors of Catholic plots. Their queen, though officially Protestant, had had a procession of flirtations with Catholic suitors, yet English sympathies were constantly being played upon over the plight of Protestant brethren across the waters. They would be called upon to participate in campaigns of liberation, only to learn in due time that these same friends had been left to fend for themselves by a half-committed queen and an overcautious administration. Now in March of 1599 the greatest expeditionary force ever to leave English shores was being assembled to pacify Ireland, a perennial trouble spot and the refuge of Spaniards and Jesuit intriguers. Appointed reluctant commander was the popular Earl of Essex, who if left to his own devices would have much preferred to continue operations in Spain on the scale of his Cadiz expedition three years before. The recruiting methods employed or condoned by the government were, as usual, scandalous, and tax riots resulted. Then from Ireland came reports of idleness and inaction and of discontent among the ranks, followed by a sudden and unauthorized return of the earl to home shores. He was put in custody and tried for mismanagement. It was the beginning of the swift decline of his fortunes. The trial took place in the summer of 1600, when Shakespeare's play was likely being set up in type, the players having been unsuccessful in forestalling its publication by a profit-seeking bookseller. It is an obvious inference that it had been played in the previous months and had been popular.

So much for political events. It is only necessary to round out the sketch with reference to the matter of present concern, censorship. Whether or not there was any strict connection—the rash of "Roman" satires and epigrams that Archbishop Whitgift attempted to put a stop to by decree on June 1, 1599, may have been merely a symptom of the general unrest—the fact remains that these were times of unusual censorship activity. There is evidence that the authorities were particularly perturbed in the summer of 1600 by "libels" circulating in London in connection with the bruited failure of the Irish campaign and with Elizabeth's alleged mistreatment of Essex. There was an effort that summer to get the justices of the city to limit the plays given by the two favored acting companies to two a week. More than once in its sittings over the Essex affair the Privy Council found itself returning with suspicion to the circumstances of the publication of a pamphlet entitled *The First Part of the Life and raigne of King Henry IIII,* written by a Dr. John Hayward the year before and provocatively, they thought, dedicated to the Earl of Essex. It is a curious coincidence that the pamphlet must have been going through the press at about the same time as Shakespeare's own *2 Henry IV,* a play that had been acted perhaps at the most three years earlier and now, with offending passages deleted, was considered fit for publication. Very likely—and the surmise has been ventured in connection with the revival of *Richard II* on the eve of Essex's rebellion—their privileged position as the Lord Chamberlain's players kept Shakespeare and his fellows out of trouble comparable to that which befell Hayward.

With this we return to the play *Henry V,* written and produced when the foregoing events were at their height, a patriotic play but one that manages to keep to its theme only at the cost of a certain lack of coherence and even credibility. Along, that is, with the elements that one might, if one chose, confuse with an exalted, superpatriotism: the scowling belligerence of the English command, the thinned ranks of English soldiery earning the sweetest of all praise—the grudging respect of an elegant well-fed army of "pros," the marvelous locker-room spirit of their leader's speeches; along with these, I say, one has to reckon with a number of elements that bulk large and incongruously: the amount of space given to comically quarreling "foreigners," who as a matter of fact also appear to be doing most of the fighting; English soldiers, when they are not represented as the scum of London, shown engaged in debating the justice of their leader's cause; the leader himself apparently riddled with doubts on the same score —these and, as I shall show, others equally discordant, make up a play that many a critic has taken to be an expression of the purest patriotism. Others have not been so sure. Am I myself stacking the cards? I do not think so, but I think Shakespeare was. I am as sure as the next that the man was a patriot. His love for his country permeates the songs that he wrote on her seasons, her sun and rain and wind. But he was also a wit and a Londoner, and he numbered among his acquaintances men who had been involved in "sedition"—Thomas Nashe was even then ending his days in Bithynian exile in Yarmouth—men, need it be said, no less patriotic than himself. That Shakespeare should have followed his unsettling play on the reign of Henry IV ("soft on rebellion" might have been an official suspicion) with a "safe" play on the reign of the great Henry V, freighting the latter with as scandalous a disrespect of Church and State as every writer indulged in in less dangerous times, may jar with notions of the sweet Shakespeare of tradition, but I cannot see that it endangers his position as a world poet. In the long view of things, there are other Chains of Being than those that bind a man to Aristotle and Aquinas. To use Samuel Coleridge's phrase, there is the "unquestioning devotion" to hearth, common, assize, and church, devotion to all that essentially conjoins man.

Before reading into *Henry V* an even greater comic "doubleness of vision" than has heretofore been suspected,[8] I propose first to establish something not generally admitted, and that is the close continuity between it and its predecessor, *2 Henry IV*. In an important sense, a publishing sense, they are even to be considered contemporaries, this despite our ignorance of who published them.

Part II of *Henry IV* was entered on the Stationer's register on August 23, 1600, *Henry V* a week earlier on August 14; the one in "good" quarto form presumably some months after its production in one of the older theatres, the other in "bad" or mangled form shortly after production at the Globe, perhaps in haste. The earlier play is unusual among Shakespeare's history plays for being accompanied by a preface, and an ambiguous one at that, called in the script "Induction." The Induction consists of a forty-line address by Rumour, an actor "painted full of tongues," half of which address divulges the events of the first scene of the new play, the other half making a commentary on the work of rumor both in general and in particular. The "in particular" deserves particular attention. In fact, it would be well to give the Induction in full, containing as it does puzzling matter that so far has escaped the attention of commentators:

Open your ears; for which of you will stop
The vent of hearing when loud Rumour speaks?
I, from the orient to the drooping west,
Making the wind my post-horse, still unfold
The acts commenced on this ball of earth:
Upon my tongues continual slanders ride,
The which in every language I pronounce,
Stuffing the ears of men with false reports.
I speak of peace, while covert enmity
Under the smile of safety wounds the world:
And who but Rumour, who but only I,
Make fearful musters and prepar'd defence,

Whilst the big year, swoln with some other grief,
Is thought with child by the stern tyrant war,
And no such matter? Rumour is a pipe
Blown by surmises, jealousies, conjectures,
And of so easy and so plain a stop
That the blunt monster with uncounted heads,
The still-discordant wavering multitude,
Can play upon it. But what need I thus
My well-known body to anatomize
Among my household? Why is Rumour here?
I run before King Harry's victory;
Who in a bloody field by Shrewsbury
Hath beaten down young Hotspur and his troops,
Quenching the flame of bold rebellion
Even with the rebels' blood. But what mean I
To speak so true at first? my office is
To noise abroad that Harry Monmouth fell
Under the wrath of noble Hotspur's sword,
And that the king before the Douglas' rage
Stoop'd his anointed head as low as death.
This have I rumour'd through the peasant towns
Between the royal field of Shrewsbury
And this worm-eaten hold of ragged stone,
Where Hotspur's father, old Northumberland,

Lies crafty-sick. The posts come tiring on,
And not a man of them brings other news
Than they have learn'd of me: from Rumour's tongues
They bring smooth comforts false, worse than true wrongs.

A stage prologue designed to anticipate, and perhaps thereby soften, a confusion prevailing in the first scene of a play at first sight bespeaks an odd lack of confidence on the part of the author either in his own ability, or his actors', to carry the burden. And here the burden is not a very large one. How significant is a rumor that does not have the slightest bearing on the play's action beyond the opening scene? (The scene itself is a bit of a puzzle in that there is nothing in Shakespeare's historical source, Holinshed, to justify the writing of it.) Rumour tells us that Henry IV and his son have not been killed; they have triumphed. It would be a very ignorant set of groundlings indeed who needed to be told that. Rumour has twenty-six and a half lines before he asks himself why he is here, six lines in which he divulges the true state of affairs, checks himself, and asks, "But what mean I/To speak so true at first?" Only then does he go on to relate the false. It is the twenty-six and a half lines that I believe bear looking into. They may be the sole and entire excuse for the Induction in the first place.

It has been suggested that the "other grief" may refer to the imminent death of the ailing king and to his continuing disappointment in his son Hal. How these can be considered a pregnancy and a pregnancy likely to be confused with warfare is a question that, to my knowledge, has never been asked. Even supposing the king's illness to be the issue of the big year, why are mustering and defense against rebellion referred to as a deception, and not simply as an additional grief? Both were verifiable truths and both public knowledge. Who is being deceived? The play that follows *is* about mustering and defense if it is about anything; the big year, dramaturgically speaking, *is* with child by the stern tyrant war (though a year's duration is a long estimate for the pacing of this particular play), and to say the contrary is not so much to whet an audience's appetite for coming complications as rather pointlessly to mislead them.

The better conjecture is that, whereas the second half of the Induction is obviously related to matter within the play, and may constitute the reason for its being spoken, the first half relates to events outside the play and constitutes the reason for its being penned.

> Whilst the big year, swoln with some other grief,
> Is thought with child by the stern tyrant war,
> *And no such matter?*

What then is the other grief from which musterings and alarms have successfully diverted attention? I think that we are almost compelled to think of matters relating to the theatre, to another summer harvest of discomfort suffered by acting companies and players over a dramatic venture, perhaps ill-timed, perhaps ill-conceived. Intended or not as a political play, politics have nevertheless intruded.[9] We recall that it was summertime, too, in 1597 when that other play of the Lord Chamberlain's players, *Richard II*, was (some believe) having a reckoning with the Privy Council during the memorable days of the *Isle of Dogs*. The possibility deserves looking into in some detail, but first I should like to have a word about rumor.

Four centuries have elapsed since the Lancaster series was written and played, and the rumor that launched the last of them is still flourishing. Put even more strongly, what are we to say of a rumor so successful that it has not even been labeled a rumor over such a stretch of years? I refer to the curtain lines of *2 Henry IV*, concluding the play with whose Induction we have just been occupied:

> I will lay odds, that, ere this year expire,
> We bear our civil swords and native fire
> As far as France. I heard a bird so sing,
> Whose music, to my thinking, pleas'd the king.

The lines are spoken by Prince John of Lancaster, whose source of information was a conversation to which he was not party. It was a conversation to which no one was party but the two participants, the dying king and his son, the Prince of Wales. (To this, we the audience are witness.) Here is the deathbed injunction of father to son:

Therefore, my Harry,
Be it thy course to busy giddy minds
With foreign quarrels; that action, hence borne out,
May waste the memory of the former days.
More would I, but my lungs are wasted so
That strength of speech is utterly denied me.
(IV, v, 211–216)

To say that the Prince listened to his injunction is one thing. To say that he concurred or gave even a moment's heed is to participate in as monstrous a slander as can be conceived against a Christian ruler, let alone an honest man. The particular time and place are not important—no more so than in the case of Thoreau's border war; it is the stark, unadorned principle. A good ruler does not open hostilities with his neighbor as a means of coping with ills at home. A good man, the microcosm of a well-ordered state, does not turn with violence upon the fellow next to him to distract attention from some disorder he harbors within himself. So much the worse, not the less, if his troubles are not of his own making. Yet Shakespeare is supposed to have written a play on such a theme. By many he is supposed to have written it in a spirit of total approval. No question but "upon my tongues continual slanders ride,/The which in every language I pronounce."

There is no difficulty, of course, for those who see in Prince Hal from the start of the plays only a chip off the old Bolingbroke block, a somewhat more interesting and complex replica of his father. "If he wasn't at the start, that's what he grew up into." Yes, in that first soliloquy of Hal's there is a touch of the Machiavel or—with a smile—"more than a little of the Florentine." Now, as Harry Monmouth, he has merely come into his own:

> . . . and at his heels,
> Leash'd in like hounds, should famine, sword, and fire
> Crouch for employment.
>
> (*Henry V, Prologue,* 6–8)

Particularly the famine.[10] The spectacle of our penitent tavern-haunter, our knightly victor at Shrewsbury, setting about this calculated task and setting about it with such apocalyptic fury has struck many as odd, certainly, but also as quite possible. All they have had to weigh against it is surely one of the most monumental silences in stage history, the Prince's silence when he accepted the assignment. Beyond that there is the inscrutability of Shakespeare.[11] And yet . . . in heaven's name why the apocalyptic rage?

But who is to be the chip off the old block if not Hal? It was a Machiavellian-conceived war, and he carried it out.

> O! for a Muse of fire, that would ascend
> The brightest heaven of invention;
> A kingdom for a stage, princes to act
> And monarchs to behold the swelling scene.
> . . . .
> But pardon, gentles all,
> The flat unraised spirits that hath dar'd
> On this unworthy scaffold to bring forth
> So great an object . . .
>
> (*Ibid.*, 1–11)

I earnestly hope that I will not be charged with facetiousness when I mention the inconspicuous John of Lancaster. Small wonder that succeeding times have given him such scant attention, a man whose role in the life of the plays is to carry out the policies of others, a moral nonentity. Yet we have to make do with what we have. At least he bears the proper name. Shakespeare followed Holinshed in giving this name to the Duke of Bedford of the plays, nothing resembling the wise and selfless administrator of France as he is known to history.

Let us give some thought to the candidacy of Prince John of Lancaster. Beyond the fact that Falstaff had an instinctive dislike for him, is there not something suspicious in this business of giving him what amount to curtain lines in two plays (both parts of *Henry IV*) and making him the connecting link with the third, of introducing him in places where Holinshed has not, of substituting him three times for another character, his veritable trademark sending better men than himself to their death? It is all summed up in this: Prince Hal, on winning the hard-fought battle of Shrewsbury, pardons prisoners of war; John, after his ghastly bloodless victory at Gaultree Forest, executes them.

This is the Lancaster who is privileged to speak for the new king on the death of the old, in lines that assure us that music of wars abroad are pleasing to the latter's ears. Rules of primogeniture notwithstanding, the direct line of descent in the Lancaster line would seem to be from Henry IV through the younger son, John, the son with the attributes that go with the name; ruthlessness, opportunism, and efficiency.[12]

A somewhat lengthy excursion into the political arena of late Tudor times is called for before we turn to the texts of the plays. In 1599–1600 the eye of the dramatist Shakespeare may have been focused upon fifteenth-century France, but that does not mean that what he saw was uncolored by events close to home. To rule this out is to deny him what we do no other author or artist, the right to have lived at a certain time in history and in a certain place. The summers of 1598 and 1599 were times of particular unrest in London. In the space of a "big" (pregnant) year, Lord Burghley had died, and the reins of government had been handed over to his physically small and somewhat misshapen son Robert Cecil; the Earl of Essex, his rival for Elizabeth's favor, found himself unwilling Lord Deputy in Ireland. One of Essex's grievances was that for his patriotic hostility to the Spanish he had come to be rumored a warmonger, and now he found himself prosecuting an unpopular war. His friend, the Earl of Southampton—Shakespeare's patron—accompanied him, doing so against the wishes of the queen.

I do not think it necessary to decide now whether Shakespeare and others of the Lord Chamberlain's players were "Essex men" (it stands to reason that they were). I am in search of a pattern of events that will help clarify a prologue and certain scenes in a play that has suspiciously political overtones. By political, I mean that which adversely affects the theatrical world. Sufficient pattern emerges from the following facts: the death of the elder statesman Burghley, a sad blow to Elizabeth, who ordered universal mourning on a scale never before seen in England; the succession of his son Robert, thought to be as deep-dyed a Machiavel as his father;[13] a popular expectation that the brilliant earl would make short work of the Irish and return to England in triumph (this despite clear official knowledge that Essex was frittering away their chances of victory—and was very likely "intriguing").

Two particular circumstances about Robert Cecil deserve attention. Like Prince John in the play, he had in effect "supplied" the place of a misbehaving favorite at the Council table. What dramatist could be wholly immune to sayings that had begun to take on the coloring of folklore:

> Not Robin Goodfellow nor Robin Hood
> But Robin the devil that never did any good?

A year before his father's death, the deserving young secretary had been made Chancellor of the Duchy of Lancaster. It is worth noting that as early as *1 Henry IV* Shakespeare had changed the identity of the younger brother who took Hal's place at the Council table from Clarence to John; Clarence it was in Holinshed, but John it is who makes a silent appearance in the opening scene of the play.

By August, when the puzzling Induction to *2 Henry IV* was being set up in type, some months had passed since Essex had been tried for his disastrous mismanagement of the Irish war and cashiered—he was hoping for the renewal of his monopoly on the sale of sweet wines (Falstaff's and Hal's "sack"), his chief source of revenue—but the Star Chamber was still pursuing the matter of theatrical libels of the previous year. Is it too much to imagine the minds of the Chamberlain's players, "sick of happiness," reverting to the summer of 1597, when the theatres were closed down because of the *Isle of Dogs,* a play put on by the rival company, the Admiral's Men? Three actors, including Ben Jonson, had gone to jail—by mere coincidence to be released on the same day that young Cecil received confirmation of his lucrative Lancaster appointment—and one had fled the city. What bird was it that had sung to the authorities that the play was seditious and slanderous? Though private news services were nothing new in Tudor England, Robert Cecil's has been vouched to have been the most far-reaching and efficient of them all.[14]

Perhaps the new history even now being rehearsed—also the quite harmless Falstaff play, *Merry Wives,* now playing—will cancel all suspicions and make everything right. No ailing Bolingbroke in this play, no shameful recruiting methods. Only tall fellows and hale are going to this war:

Yoke-fellows in arms,
Let us to France; like horse-leeches, my boys,

To suck, to suck, the very blood to suck!
(*Henry V*, II, iii, 57–59)

"I speak of peace," said Rumour, "while covert enmity/ Under the smile of safety wounds the world." Well, let it be war then, to busy giddy minds and waste the memory of the former days—but a good war, one to which not a person can possibly object.

There is no reason to suppose Shakespeare was on intimate terms with the head of state who was his patron's friend. But the Earl of Essex, unlike Robert Cecil, was not a secretive person—as we know from his extant letters. The following passages, however, are from a formal *Apologie* composed for friends in 1598. That a few copies reached print in 1600 was, according to the Earl, the work of an unscrupulous bodyservant.

> The reputation of a most faithful subject and zealous Patriot . . . must not suffer this oughly and odious aspersion, *that my actions haue caused, mainteined, or increased the warres, or had euer any such scope or intent.*

Challenging his critics to show that his "affection to peace" was in any way founded on insincerity, he suggested that:

. . . these rules which I avow to hold in Iudgement to be compared to the doctrin of some Diuines of our time, furthest of all from their practice.[15]

The passage may shed light on the prominent role played by an Archbishop and subordinate clerics in the opening scene of *Henry V*—though again Shakespeare found plenty of support in Holinshed for the warlike nature of divines.

The famous Chorus launching the concluding act of *Henry V*, in describing the return of the hero to England, compares the excitement of it to that which would attend the arrival of the Earl of Essex were he to return from Ireland now:

How many would the peaceful city quit
To welcome him! much more, and much more cause,
Did they this Harry.

(33–35)

As we are very shortly to see for ourselves, Harry Monmouth, unlike the belligerent earl, was a profoundly peaceful man. No question of warmongering in that quarter!

3

The rather lengthy proceedings thus far will have been justified if what follows falls into place simply and naturally. The central and never sufficiently emphasized fact is that Shakespeare's Harry Monmouth is *not* the historical victor of Agincourt, that splendid and humane uniter of two kingdoms, and indeed the only Henry V that Shakespeare's contemporaries could have known about or believed in. (An Appendix containing excerpts from Holinshed will suggest what traits a truer portrait might have contained had Shakespeare cared to develop them.) The portrait Shakespeare has given us is of a man *not pleased* with the task laid upon him—of carrying fire and sword into another country. The obvious inference is that *Shakespeare* was not pleased. No matter if he exaggerated; the degree of his exaggeration is an index of his displeasure. I ask the reader to entertain the hypothesis while I review with him the key scenes of the play. Much of what I point out will not be new (it will be different when I come to *Henry IV*), but with the aid of the hypothesis, the total may for once be made to amount to something.

The difficulty inherent in the play *Henry V* is probably traceable to the very nature of burlesque. Harry is a walking embodiment of personal pacifism and institutional belligerence; indeed the playwright's gusto in detailing the horrors of war, vying with his insistence that they are none of the new king's doing, leaves it very much in doubt who is responsible for all the bloody thoughts. Nor has the belligerence any likely object to vent itself on, the French on the whole being presented as a rather reasonable lot, in fact rather English. Lastly, for one with an ear for such differences, it must be said that not all of Harry's lines are equally objectionable. Some obviously go with the good old tradition of chivalry. Taken with certain frank references to an all too recent reform, they may very well represent traces of an original play, in the making at the time when the regrettable incidents already documented at such length intruded and forced the author's hand.

Act I opens with the Bishop of Ely and the Archbishop of Canterbury discussing the wonderful change wrought in their sovereign by the death of his father. Concealed in the high-sounding language is mockery certainly as great as that described by Francis Fergusson in the Murder of Gonzago playlet of *Hamlet*.[16] The clerics pass from Henry's sanctity, in which he outchurches the Church, to his diplomacy:

> Turn him to any cause of policy,
> The Gordian knot of it he will unloose,
> Familiar as his garter; that, when he speaks,
> The air, a charter'd libertine, is still,

And the mute wonder lurketh in men's ears,
To steal his sweet and honey'd sentences.
(45–50)

Precious little evidence of this is there in the course of the play! From his vehement opening charge to themselves—and what biting irony this!—that they forego the customary casuistical "wresting" of texts and honestly interpret his claims to France—to the boisterous wooing of Kate toward the end of the play, there is little either of the serpent or of the dove in Harry to warrant him any sort of a rating in diplomacy. As for the particular "cause of policy" now in question, both the repeated declaration that it is they who are doing the inciting to war, not he, and the eventual refusal to take even an iota of credit for the victory, pretty clearly show the turnabout of roles that the playwright was effecting—"a parody of ritual," again to quote Fergusson. It is a turnabout indeed when the secular finds itself warning of the inhumane consequences of an action, the spiritual assuaging inconvenient scruples:

Gracious lord,
Stand for your own; unwind your bloody flag;
Look back into your mighty ancestors!
(I, ii, 100–102)

Yes, undoubtedly the Church knows best about such things, just as it knows best which of ones plays contain politically dangerous or subversive matter. Incidentally, it is to be remarked that there is no talk here of Harry's going to France to keep the peace, the reason he tries to give himself on the eve of the battle of Agincourt.

Much has been made by critics of the aptness and beauty of the beehive image by dint of which the clerics convince the new king that he will be leaving an ordered and peaceful realm behind him. (Essex on his way to Ireland had considerable doubts on this score.) Looking for isolated beauties in Shakespeare is not an occupation to be entirely discouraged, but on this occasion I second the recommendation of R. L. Stevenson, who felt that more than any playwright Shakespeare should be read symphonically. Reread the beehive passage for the express purpose of contrasting its pleasant cadences with the businesslike vigor of the King's reply:

> Call in the messengers sent from the Dauphin.
> Now are we well resolv'd; and by God's help,
> And yours, the noble sinews of our power,
> France being ours, we'll bend it to our awe
> Or break it all to pieces. . . .
>
> (*Ibid.*, 221–225)

As Prince of Wales, he must have had to listen to many such discourses by his father's councillors. Eventually, his place was taken by a more attentive younger brother. I should not be surprised if Shakespeare found them tedious too, though he wrote a much longer one in *Troilus and Cressida* that has been even more admired than this. In any case, he has left it open to us to take note that none of the speakers in the above scene shows any concern for how the other fellow may feel about *his* beehive.[17]

For readers unacquainted with Shakespeare's historical sources, I must make it clear that none of the savagery to follow can be laid to Holinshed. Holinshed is not bloodthirsty. We see in his pages a Henry who never indulged in gratuitous "brags," who never offered extremes of violence to the foe until such had first been offered to him, and who was finally brought to make peace from a natural desire to preserve his patrimony rather than to continue to destroy it.[18] Even in the notorious episode of the order given at Agincourt to cut the French prisoners' throats, to which we shall be coming presently, Holinshed stated categorically that it was given by Henry "contrarie to his accustomed gentlenes."[19] Shakespeare's systematic ignoring of these features of his chief source should long ago have made someone curious about what he thought he was accomplishing. His Monmouth, for example, is not merely a man easily provoked, but a man almost insanely provoked. The very thought of being crossed in the slightest degree sends this wielder of "sweet and honey'd sentences" (so said the Archbishop) into paroxysms of rage. The whole seems to me a fairly obvious parody of the behavior of the benevolent despot: I offer only fairness and civility, and what is my return? If we recall the image of the offensive wife and her enraged husband in *2 Henry IV*, it brings to mind something about "restraint" exercised in the face of "grossest provocation."

Before modern criticism was sharpening its tools, the stupendous violence of Henry V's language allowed the older critics only two choices, either to ignore it as having no particular significance in a war play, or to attribute it to some anticipation of later British imperialism. The time is past when a critic noted both for good sense and humor can pen such a passage as the following and not see that he is himself writing parody:

> . . . and then follows a picture of violence and licentiousness let loose such as would be hard to duplicate in Shakepeare: bloody soldiers seizing by the hair still-shrieking virgins, old men with their brains dashed out against the walls, naked infants spitted upon pikes, mothers run mad as in the days of Herod . . .[20]

For the sake of contrast he goes on to quote another passage from Act III:

> And we give express charge, that in our marches through the country, there be nothing compelled from the villages, nothing taken but paid for, none of the French upbraided or abused in disdainful language; for when lenity and cruelty play for a kingdom, the gentler gamester is the soonest winner.[21]

The contrast, of course, reveals the Lancastrian hypocrite, the despoiler of France now about to acquiesce villainously in the execution of his "old friend" Bardolph for stealing a trifle from a church. On the contrary, what I see are two images of the national soul, both realizable, both possible. One may smash the other fellow's beehive and preserve his own, or one may preserve both.

> The soul recovers radical innocence
> And learns at last that it is self-delighting,
> Self-appeasing, self-affrighting,
> And that its own sweet will is Heaven's will.

But with the advent of modern criticism, Yeats's solar times are in full swing. For Professor Traversi, Shakespeare's Harry Monmouth is merely a Tudor executive-in-training. The frightful violence of his language can be explained as promising the "unnatural" self-control or "impersonality" required of rulers in the new Europe that Shakespeare saw in the making. Both the "grotesque inhumanity" of it and his indifference to suffering are excused on the grounds that they have something to do with a "sense of the tragedy of the royal position." [22] If I make anything of this thought, it is perhaps the existential one that a sovereign's duty was once to pass on the discomforts of his position to those under him rather than try to shield them from them. Can the prevalence, or even the existence, of such a doctrine in the past be convincingly documented? If not, I think it a little unfair to saddle it on Shakespeare.

The most extreme instance of Harry's inhumanity is the one already cited in connection with Goddard's strictures, involving the stubborn citizens of the French town of Harfleur. Here it is simpler to place Henry's language where it belongs, among the oldest pretenses in the despot's baggage—that in the event of victory he cannot be sure of controlling his soldiery, more precisely, cannot "promise" to control them. As for any intention on Harry's part of finding tragic responsibility in kingship, I am at a loss to see any trace of it in the rather swashbuckling passage in which he announces that, after his present "plodding" days as a soldier are over, he intends to enjoy sway and domination to the utmost:

> But tell the Dolphin I will keep my state,
> Be like a king, and show my sail of greatness,

When I do rouse me in my throne of France.

. . . .

. . . I will rise there with so full a glory
That I will dazzle all the eyes of France—
Yea, strike the Dolphin blind to look on us.

(I, ii, 273–280)

In the next chapter we shall explore quite fully the bearing of this sun imagery on the outlook of the present monarch when he was the heir apparent, Prince Hal. There I am indeed confident that we shall find something approaching the consciousness of responsibility that I, for one, find lacking in the above.[23]

Outright contradictions, of course, go to make up this play. Take Henry's words at the approach of the French ambassadors:

Or there we'll sit
Ruling in large and ample empery
O'er France . . .

. . . or else our grave,
Like Turkish mute, shall have a tongueless mouth,
Not worshipp'd with a waxen epitaph.

(*Ibid.* 225–233)

Caesar or nothing! A strange admission from one who the next moment will invite the French to approach in manly fearlessness:

We are no tyrant, but a Christian king;
Unto whose grace our passion is as subject
As is our wretches fetter'd in our prisons.
(*Ibid.*, 241–243)

As Traversi remarks, such self-control is "necessarily precarious," [24] and Henry's soon-to-be-demonstrated inability to take a joke will cost many a Frenchwoman her husband. "Tensions" of this kind, however, catch the eye less at the moment than the reference to a Turkish mute and to fettered prisoners. Recalling the professed horror of Elizabeth's subjects at conditions prevailing in autocratic Turkey, we should at the same time recall the wonder of a Venetian ambassador at the more than Turkish servility that Elizabeth demanded of her court even on minor state occasions.

We next go directly to what for some has been the crux of the play, Henry's order for the cutting of the French prisoners' throats. Controversy[25] has narrowed to the question of who committed the barbarity first, French or English, and to whether the scene is designed to show Henry's beastliness or merely to show that that is what "war is like." The author holding the latter viewpoint even went to the trouble of consulting army officers, who assured him that there was really not time enough in the stage interval provided by Shakespeare to slaughter very many prisoners, so perhaps only a token few were done in and, for realism, on the stage. We learn something about the temperaments of critics from this sort of thing, but the important point is missed, that a very short and hurried reference to the deed gives rise to a conversation of some duration, and of greater import, a colloquy between two representative soldiers who discuss the implications of the deed. Stout Gower—or should it be "honest" Gower?—says:

> 'Tis certain, there's not a boy left alive; and the cowardly rascals that ran from the battle have done this slaughter: besides, they have burned and carried away all that was in the king's tent; wherefore the king most worthily hath caused every soldier to cut his prisoner's throat. O! 'tis a gallant king.
> (IV, vii, 5–11)

To which Fluellan answers, "Ay, he was porn at Monmouth, Captain Gower." Then begins the exoneration of Henry for the "killing" of Falstaff—a subject he broaches himself—on the grounds that Alexander "the Pig," who killed his friend Cleitus, was born by a salmon-bearing river in Macedonia as Henry had had been in Wales by the river Wye. "I'll tell you, there is goot men porn at Monmouth," concludes the Welshman.

All this seems like pretty heavy allusion from our vantage point. We cannot even guess how much, if any, of it was expected to get across to the original audiences. It is different with the words spoken directly to Henry when the latter appeared to proclaim the victory. All the winning Welsh bluster in the world does not conceal the fact that a kinship is being claimed of a sort that one would as soon disown, depending as it does on one's being found honest:

> All the water in Wye cannot wash your majesty's Welsh plood out of your pody, I can tell you that; . . . By Jeshu, I am your majesty's countryman, I care not who know it; I will confess it to all the 'orld: I need not be ashamed of your majesty, praised be God, so long as your majesty is an honest man.
>
> KING HENRY. God keep me so!
>
> (*Ibid.*, 112–122)

Need not be ashamed of his Majesty! Or of her present Majesty? The effrontery of it is chilling. We are reminded of the conversations of Gulliver with the Brobdingnagian king and of Gulliver's hopeless efforts to remove from the latter's mind the false notions of Europeans put there by the author himself. Jonathan Swift, of course, ventured little when he indulged in such humor; between Shakespeare and the most fearful of consequences there stood only his own calculation of the astuteness of licensers and a tenuous ecology of the river Wye. Men of their discernment must be weary of dainty and such picking grievances! Let them exercise themselves on this.

Has it been noted before that Gower, with whom Fluellan opened the conversations above summarized, was cast by Shakespeare in the role of a toady? Briefly introduced in *2 Henry IV* as the social superior of Falstaff, Gower is there toadied to by Falstaff, as Falstaff in turn is toadied to by Shallow, Shallow by Silence. . . . Now in *Henry V* it falls to Gower to toady to his king with an offer of humankind's most abysmal praise; ". . . to cut his prisoners' throats. O! 'tis a gallant king!" Henry—"God's substitute"— was not there to hear it. If I may be permitted a blasphemy, neither may God himself have been very close at hand on those innumerable other occasions (so sought after and described by a learned branch of modern criticism) to hear the praise ascending to Him from Throne and Pulpit.[26]

There is nothing ambiguous about the next scene to be discussed, and many of my remarks have been anticipated by others. The scene is that of the "little touch of Harry in the night," the long discussion by the disguised king with three of his soldiers about the justice of the cause they are fighting for. Others have pointed out that Harry declines to answer the questions put to him and shifts to safer topics, and they have generally deplored the poor light in which he is made to appear. Some have pointed out that the prose itself is "wooden." My only contribution will be to suggest again a reading of the whole in closer association with the following scene, one that shows the deep uneasiness that such questioning arouses in him.

The challenge put to him by his men is this: in view of the dangers to which common soldiers are exposed in warfare, will not a king's responsibility be a very heavy one, if the cause he enlists them in is found not to be a just one? It was a tactless question to broach on the eve of one of the better accredited—Fluellan would say "honest"—military engagements of history, and Henry's answer can hardly avoid being what it is, a rather undignified dodge. (Can he tell them about the Salic Law?) He takes the perfectly plain and clear import of soldiers' "not dying well" to mean dying "with sins on their consciences," and about this he is very eloquent indeed. He concludes rightly that no king can be responsible for the state of his subjects' souls; that is their concern. One of his interlocutors, John Bates, a good little man like Feeble, the ladies' tailor, in *2 Henry IV*, says he will do his duty anyway, but Michael Williams does not let his liege lord off so easily. He answers sarcastically, " 'Tis certain, every man that dies ill, the ill upon his own head: the king is not to answer for it." Henry may shift ground again, but it makes no difference to Williams. To the remark that Henry has heard the King say himself that he will not let himself be ransomed in the event of a defeat,

Williams answers, "Ay, he said so, to make us fight cheerfully; but when our throats are cut he may be ransomed, and we ne'er the wiser." Yes, an unfortunate possibility. Williams, no more than Falstaff, is able to tell a king in the dark by instinct, but unlike Falstaff he did not change his story the next day. And need we suppose that he was overly impressed with his reward of a glove full of gold—for what, for not being afraid?

Shakespeare did his Harry the justice of having him spend a wakeful night after this colloquy with his men. He wrestles with the thought of the well-fed and rested "lackey" who will "rise and help Hyperion to his horse" on the morrow (read Williams for the lackey, since it had been he who last applied sun imagery to his king, to the latter's annoyance), yet comforts himself after this aggressive thought by recalling the service he is performing:

> The slave, a member of the country's peace,
> Enjoys it; but in gross brain little wots
> What watch the king keeps to maintain the peace,
> Whose hours the peasant best advantages.
>
> (IV, i, 301–304)

The reflection might apply on other occasions but hardly on this, when Henry is in France taking advantage of an interpretation of the Salic Law, not maintaining his or any other country's peace.

A further word about the evasions with which Henry has met the challenge of his men. We owe to Lily Campbell our knowledge that the questions they raised were precisely those raised years before by a Catholic cardinal at the time of the English intervention against the Spanish in the Netherlands. Because Elizabeth had been excommunicated by Rome, so went the argument, no war she might thereafter undertake could be a just one, and she was cruelly endangering the souls of the men whom she was requiring to fight it—incidentally, the Dutch she was "defending" were Spanish subjects.[27] Perhaps in the strict scholarly view of things, Shakespeare's reviving of these arguments in 1599 merely attests to the strength of influences still carrying over from his youth, but to let it go at that is to skirt a large and bitter irony. It is not now intriguing Jesuits who are broaching these subtleties of natural law and conscience, but honest English foot soldiers! And though the answer they receive is substantially the same as the one that officially served in years past: "There are two 'justices' involved; you attend to yours, the monarch will attend to hers"—an answer blessedly lamed by Henry in the telling—the underlying and poignant state of affairs is not so easily silenced. For who *is* to concern himself with English souls in the new, centralized Elizabethan settlement? Who is to point out to Englishmen, among other things, that there is more to war than winning it or staying out of it? In the spectacle of the other fellow's house burned, his wife outraged, his children orphaned, his crops ruined, is there no room for other emotions than the congratulatory ones—none for pity? In the present play it is more than a patriotic Frenchman who speaks the touching lines of Burgundy in the last act:

> Why that the naked, poor, and mangled Peace,
> Dear nurse of arts, plenties, and joyful births,
> Should not in this best garden of the world,
> Our fertile France, put up her lovely visage?
> (V, ii, 34–37)

The mere naming of the weeds that have overgrown the land brings to mind *Lear,* for the catalogue, "darnell, hemlock and rank fumitory," is nearly the same as that with which the old king was decking himself, in the last stages of his madness, when he was discovered by Cordelia. Even now, it is possible that Shakespeare's mind had conceived the outlines of another play, one in which an invasion of one nation by another is undertaken in selfless love. The leader will be a woman—a dove of peace, yet with a good element of iron strength in her.

I cannot find much to say for the "God-of-battles" prayer with which the entire night episode concludes. Shakespeare had had a score of opportunities in previous scenes here and in other plays to drop the suggestion that the son of Henry IV suffered pangs of guilt for the family past. On the contrary, he might by now have been a little tired of the contemporary cant about the sins of one's political forebears. One has faults enough of one's own to be attended to, if at all, by "heart's sorrow/ And a clear life ensuing." He had read with his own eyes in his Holinshed the author's statement that the blame for Richard's death deserved to be shared by the usurper's subjects "sithens they were so readie to joine and clappe hands with him, for the deposing of their rightfull and naturall prince king Richard, whose cheefe fault rested onlie in that, that he was too bountifull to his freends, and too mercifull to his foes." [28] If—as it should have been—Harry Monmouth's mind had been on the state of affairs that compliance with his father's ministers had brought him to, he would be having quite other thoughts: should he win against the frightful odds of the morrow, at best he would only be vindicating God's concern for correct interpretations of the Salic Law; should he lose, God forbid, there would be ringing in his ears the voices of thousands upon thousands of ghostly Williamses. To conclude, considering the absence of any deeper undercurrent of feeling supplied by earlier scenes, I think the God-of-battles soliloquy is more aptly read as having reference to contemporary Lancastrian guilts than to any inherited from the past. If the simple soul of Monmouth experienced such twinges, how much more should those of persons alive now in England! [29]

The final episode to be taken up is for me conclusive evidence that Shakespeare was less concerned with plumbing royal psychology than he was with dissociating his king from the conscious insincerities of contemporary official mythology.[30] What he gives us is historically quite incredible. Prince John of Lancaster, on winning his battle at Gaultree Forest, had cried, "God, and not we, hath safely fought to-day." After Agincourt Henry echoes the sentiment, but echoes it with a sort of holy ferocity:

> And be it death proclaimed through our host
> To boast of this or take the praise from God
> Which is His only.
>
> (IV, viii, 119–121)

It is impossible to dismiss this as just chronicle matter—or worse, Christian piety. In Holinshed there is a decent refusal to take credit, *Non Nobis,* but no threatening of penalties, certainly not death! As for piety, the spectacle of a charismatic hero renouncing with superstitious fury any part in his charisma is like no other piety that has been seen on the face of the earth. A better name for it is irony. To give God absolute and undisputed credit for the slaughter of ten thousand Frenchmen at the cost of twenty-five English ("But other writers of greater credit affirme, that there were slaine above five or six hundred" [31]) may very well have been Shakespeare's final gesture of cooperation with Archbishop Whitgift and his Ecclesiastic Commission. "Take it, God,/ For it is none but thine!" [32] (IV, viii, 115–116).

Except for the long and touching speech by a Frenchman already partly quoted, the play for our purposes ends here. Much of Act V is taken up with comedy, like Falstaff in love, of no very high order. To ask what stability is guaranteed a land whose monarch woos his queen—emblem of the union of Christ and his Church—in the language of a loutish carter[33] wooing a shy woman of property is to certify oneself as lacking in humor. One of the promises made in the Epilogue to *2 Henry IV* had been in the next play to "make you merry with fair Katherine of France."

4

We have completed the exposure of the travesty promised at the outset of the chapter; it remains to count the cost. Let us remind ourselves, however, that it is a bookkeeping of small interest to the multitudes who have enjoyed the play for its many dramatic merits and will continue to enjoy it, now as in Shakespeare's day. It is to a minority who have come to regard *Henry V* as a badly flawed play that I feel I owe a word of consolation for having confirmed their feelings and if anything made things worse. I do not flatter myself that the sense of loss they sustain on leaving their once bright denizen of Eastcheap talking to Katherine of France as he never talked to Dame Quickly or Doll Tearsheet is compensated for by the discovery of a potential Voltaire in the author.

I offer, therefore, this consolation: the work is a travesty, and Harry Monmouth is still Prince Hal but Prince Hal in disguise. He is in disguise in the same way and to the same degree as Edgar was throughout most of *King Lear*. I hope it is not straining things too far to say that the very unnaturalness of his behavior testifies to his creator's tenacious hold on the ideal, and the ideal is the important thing.

> The Prince has been drawn with special affection. It even seems probable that the author was describing himself in many respects. . . . The prince is in complete contrast to his father; he is so clearly conscious of his high position, that he exuberantly throws dignity to the winds. . . . Like a true Briton, the prince likes, next to deep earnestness, nothing so much as wit and humour.

> The Prince, as the Poet conceives him, is of a profoundly good and generous nature: gentle and forceful, energetic and

gracious, expansive and reserved, indulgent and yet firm, modest and brave and serene.[34]

These, I take it, are the expressions of persons—one a German, the other a Frenchman—who have, as it were, seen through the disguise. (Judging from the eight pages of character appreciation devoted to Hal in the Variorum edition of *1 Henry IV* it would seem obligatory not to be an Englishman, or an Irishman with British imperialism on his mind, truly to "appreciate" Hal.)

Here then we have a Prince who, fictively speaking, never died. Surely the answer to the inevitable question, why did not Shakespeare write a death scene for his Monmouth, is: Why should he have—he never believed in him in the first place. Monmouth vanishes from our sight speaking schoolboy French to the mother of the unfortunate Henry VI, as finally as did Poins, his evil reflection, in the play *2 Henry IV*.

The only heroic characters drawn to live in good memory in the play we have been reading—unless we wish to recall the glorious parting-in-death of York and Suffolk in Act IV—are a handful of young Frenchmen who relieved the tedium of waiting for the dawn of Agincourt with the age-old banter of youth:

. . . *le cheval volant,* the Pegasus, *qui a les narines de feu!*
When I bestride him, I soar, I am a hawk: he trots the air;

the earth sings when he touches it; the basest horn of his hoof is more musical than the pipe of Hermes. . . .

ORLEANS. Your mistress bears well.

DAUPHIN. Me well; which is the prescript praise and perfection of a good and particular mistress.

Or:

ORLEANS. Ay, but these English are shrewdly out of beef.

CONSTABLE. Then shall we find to-morrow they have only stomachs to eat and none to fight. Now is it time to arm; come, shall we about it?

(III, vii, 14–53; 159–163)

These were the attractive young men who invaded the wooden "O" of the Globe on an afternoon of 1599, to put, I should say, the various native "types" to mild shame. The play was never written that brought them face to face on the comic stage with their English counterparts, Mercutio, Romeo, Benvolio—where if they had killed each other, God forbid, it would not have been for want of a "Now, lads . . ." of a Lord Chief Justice. We can imagine them if we choose—with no help from Shakespeare—among the shadowy forces that invaded England with Cordelia, just as we can imagine the stouter sort of Englishman, a Bates, a Williams, and a lady's tailor misnamed "Feeble," on the other side in the English ranks. In every country there are and always have been good men. "An't be my destiny, so; an't be not, so. No man's too good to serve's prince."

Unlike these, however, the true Harry Monmouth never came even briefly to light. He never ruled in England. Much less did he conquer France. To see who and what he *might* have been, to see him in the making "in the hatch and brood of time," we must go back to the earlier plays, *Richard II* and the two parts of *Henry IV*.

Notes to Chapter 1

1: *P. 5.* Alfred Hart, *Shakespeare and the Homilies* (Melbourne, Melbourne University Press, 1934). Hart reached his conclusion by a numerical count of the appearances in Shakespeare's writings of the Tudor doctrine of passive obedience that very likely had been instilled in him in his youth. The count being found to exceed that of any other Elizabethan dramatist (*ibid.*, pp. 73–76), it followed that he surpassed them all in orthodoxy. He must have been a royalist par excellence. Hart's essay has had an incalculable effect on a generation of scholars. Yet in the 2 *Henry IV* issue, it makes no effort to reconcile the discrepant facts of the playwright's supposed orthodoxy and his incaution in penning matter "expressed or implied, subversive of . . . basic principles" and sufficient to bring "the whole system of Tudor despotism crumbling into ruins" (*ibid.*, pp. 207, 208). Hart himself does not make the astounding inference that Shakespeare condoned the censor's deletions and perhaps considered his play improved by them, but on the other hand he does not specifically exclude it. The matter is not of trivial importance if we accept the opinion of textual critics who believe that 2 *Henry IV* is one of the plays Shakespeare saw to press himself. See Leo Kirschbaum, *Shakespeare and the Stationers* (Columbus, Ohio State University Press, 1955), pp. 165–168, for a summary of arguments for believing the first quarto to have been set up from the author's own, not the company, copy.

2: *P. 6.* Walter Wilson Greg's conclusion, after a review of the *2 Henry IV* "censorship theory"—that it all "looks very like a mare's-nest" (*The Shakespeare First Folio*, New York, Oxford University Press, 1955, pp. 273–275)—may have resulted from his having concentrated exclusively on the "Richard" excisions (see Note 29 for a conjecture about the latter). The excised passages that first interested me, the rebels' speeches, he dismisses as "unquestionably long-winded"—in other words, good candidates for the actors' own deleting. Technical arguments about the possibility of there being mislaid in the print shop a sheet containing Act III, Scene i (J. H. Smith, *Shakespeare Quarterly*, XV [1964], 173–179), should not, of course, influence our feelings about other problematical scenes, for example, Act IV, Scene i, which are *not* subject to such conjecture.

3: *P. 9.* It has probably been remarked before that the ambiguity with which the turncoat Stanley is treated in *Richard III* may reflect the circumstance that his most recent descendant was patron of the company for whom Shakespeare was then writing. *His* father in turn had been Lord Lieutenant of Lancashire and one of the commissioners who had tried Mary of Scotland (see Note 29). In *Richard III*, Stanley was not accorded the instrumental role given him by history in the victory of Elizabeth's grandfather at Bosworth Field.

4: *P. 12.* Paul Jorgensen, "The 'Dastardly Treachery' of Prince

John of Lancaster," *PMLA,* LXXVI (1961), demonstrates the growing frequency of treacherous practices on both sides in Tudor warfare. As usual with such historical research, Shakespeare emerges as no more than a "man of his times."

5: *P. 12.* E. M. W. Tillyard, *Shakespeare's History Plays* (London, 1944), p. 305.

6: *P. 16.* Arthur P. Rossiter sees behind all the histories "pathos, derision, a sad wry smile, and a malicious grin . . . and all 'belong'," "Ambivalence: The Dialectic of the Histories," *Talking of Shakespeare,* ed. John Garrett (London, 1954), p. 160.

7: *P. 19.* Quoted by Tillyard as an instance of doctrines that "battered" at Shakespeare in his youth and "captured" him. "They became as it were his official interest, the interest that his adolescent conscience took most seriously" (*op. cit.,* pp. 143–144). Is it possible that this impression too, like Hart's, is founded on a count of passages?

8: *P. 24.* Rossiter, *loc cit.* Others who have seen this doubleness of vision and in *Henry V* have assigned it to the comic rather than the tragic domain are William Empson and R. W. Battenhouse.

9: *P. 29.* In "Shakespeare, Hayward, and Essex," *PMLA,* XLV (1930), Ray Heffner can find no evidence that the Chamberlain's players were in the least involved in the Star Chamber inquiries into the libels circulating London in the summer of 1599, some of these libels (he surmises) being in reality improvised dramatizations of Hayward's book in "open houses and streets" (pp. 779–780). This, I believe, we can at least question. The facts are these: a play containing an Induction that speaks of "covert enmity/ Under the smile of safety wound [ing] the world" was not reprinted again in Elizabeth's reign. The subject of that play was one that had involved others in serious trouble. What are some inferences? The only "smile of safety" is of course that of Prince John's at Gaultree Forest. (We shall have to overlook the short duration of the "covert enmity" exhibited there.) But even *were* the Induction alluding to that episode, it could only be for the purpose of encouraging application to events *outside* the play. To worry about points being missed *inside* a play would be the mark of a production so amateurish as not to be worth the study. I offer a conjecture for what it is worth; perhaps the Chamberlain's company accepted assurances of an amnesty from the administration if they would cooperate in avoiding further libels. Whether they cooperated or did not, the offer could be felt as and construed as "wounding" the theater world. I take the word of Margaret Dowling, "Sir John Hayward's Troubles," *Library*, Series 4, XI (1930–1931), that Hayward's description of Bolingbroke's behavior ("which the seuerer sort accompt abasement," p. 219) when he was wooing the favor of the populace is nowhere matched except in Shakespeare. Nothing similar is found in Halle, Hayward's confessed source, or in any other chronicler.

10: ***P. 31.*** Shakespeare may not have approved of his government's policy of starving the Irish for purposes of political control, not sharing the view of the majority of his countrymen that the Irish were little better than cattle. (He was ahead of his times in many other ways.) At any rate, the threat of famine against the French was not something he read in his Holinshed, where Henry's warning was limited to "blood, sword, and fire" (*Chronicles: Henry* V, Oxford, 1923, p. 16). Famine comes up in a different context. At the siege of Rouen, the English, having reduced the city to starvation, found themselves burdened with numbers of citizens whom the French themselves had driven without the gates. These Henry fed, "mooved with pitie, upon Christmasse daie, in the honor of Christes Nativitie" (*ibid.,* p. 76). In answer to the French charge of inhumanity, he answered grimly that "whereas the gaine of a capteine atteined by anie of the said three handmaidens [blood, fire, and famine], was both glorious, honourable, and woorthie of triumph: yet of all the three, the youngest maid, which he meant to use at that time was most profitable and commodious" (*ibid.,* pp. 78–79).

11: ***P. 32.*** The resort to war to solve domestic problems, Paul Jorgensen points out (*Shakespeare's Military World,* University of California Press, 1956, p. 181), was not a policy ever publicly avowed. Shakespeare may have learned it from Dudley Digges's *Foure Paradoxes or Discourses.* Jorgensen notes that Bolingbroke is Shakespeare's only historical character to adopt it (*ibid.*, p. 185).

12: *P. 33.* To the objection that Prince John represents too small a part to bear the weight of so much political innuendo, two things must be said. Insofar as there was any conscious political subversion in acting companies, it may have been a greater satisfaction to see one's points scored in a printed quarto, to be perused by the like-minded at their leisure, than to have the lines actually spoken. If they were spoken (and I have been told by a native of that country that "incredible" things are said on the contemporary Polish stage), let us be reminded that the manner of speaking would have been arranged during rehearsals. Shakespeare was an actor-director and, in consultation with his associates, he had the ever-recurrent choice of heightening, muting, or omitting entirely any lines he chose in any play—and of inventing business to go with the lines, something that we seem to take for granted only in the case of comedy. At any rate, the inherited notion of an Olympian, enigmatic Shakespeare must go! *He was present at rehearsals.*

13: *P. 35.* P. M. Handover, *The Second Cecil, 1563–1604* (London, 1959), p. 316.

14: *P. 36.* See the letter from Anthony Bacon to Essex, December 20, 1596, quoted by Handover (*ibid.*, p. 176): ". . . if a public minister's letters to a king, his master, and the king's to him, have been laid in wait for, and opened, how much more letters betwixt friends." Handover summarizes: "There was too much that was uncanny for his contemporaries to stomach. When, through his news service, he came as near as any in his age to putting a girdle around the earth in forty minutes, when he effortlessly slid into other men's minds, they feared and distrusted an inhuman—or unhuman—versatility" (*ibid.*, p. 34).

15: *P. 38.* *An Apologie Of The Earle Of Essex, Against Those Which Iealovsly, And Maliciously, Tax Him To Be The Hinderer of The Peace And Quiet Of His Country. Penned by Himself in Anno 1598.* London. Imprinted by Richard Bradock, 1603, A_2v, A_3v. For Essex the disease of Spanish encroachment justified the measures of medical science: "*Excellent mindes should come to the warres, as Surgeons doe to their Cauteries,* when no other easie or ordinarie remedie will serue: or as men which haue no way but by the sworde to proue the truth of their plea, and obtaine their detained right" (A_3r).

16: *P. 40.* *The Idea of a Theatre* (Princeton, Princeton University Press, 1949), p. 124.

17: *P. 43.* Apparently I, ii, 222–225 impressed someone in Shakespeare's lifetime, for they are the only lines from *Henry V* to appear in the so-called Dering MS., a script dating from sometime after 1613 (see *A New Variorum Edition of II Henry IV*, ed. Matthias A. Shaaber, Philadelphia, 1941, p. 650) which combines portions of *1* and *2 Henry IV*, seemingly for private performance.

18: ***P. 43.*** The most menacing words spoken in Holinshed are spoken by the Archbishop, viz., ". . . destroie the people, waste the countrie, and subvert the townes with blood, sword, and fire, and never cease till he had recovered his ancient right and lawful patrimonie"—though indeed Henry "promised to performe it to the uttermost" (*Henry V*, p. 16). Compare: "But here note (by the waie) the roiall hart of this king, who as he tempered all his actions with singular circumspection; so with a pitifull mind he pondered the miserie of his enimies; so that when he might (*Iure belli*, by the law of armes) have spoiled them of goods and life, he diverse times spared both; with clemencie commonlie making conquest of them, who seemed by open hostilitie scarse conquerable (*ibid.*, p. 126).

19: ***P. 43.*** ". . . contrarie to his accustomed gentlenes, commanded by sound of trumpet, that everie man (upon paine of death) should incontinentlie slaie his prisoner" (*ibid.*, p. 38).

20: ***P. 44.*** Harold C. Goddard, *The Meaning of Shakespeare* (Chicago, University of Chicago Press, 1951), p. 237.

21: ***P. 45.*** *Ibid.*, p. 239.

22: ***P. 46.*** Derek A. Traversi, *An Approach to Shakespeare,*

2nd ed. (Garden City, N.Y., Doubleday Anchor Books, 1956), pp. 42, 40, 41 respectively.

23: *P. 47.* The accompanying references to his misspent youth may seem a little too *heavy* for the originally more light-hearted play posited on p. 40.

24: *P. 48.* Traversi, *op. cit.*, p. 37.

25: *P. 48.* William Empson, "Falstaff and Mr. Dover Wilson," *Kenyon Review*, XV (1953).

26: *P. 51.* The view that Shakespeare would condone a massacre simply because it was ordered by a king's son I take to be the *ne plus ultra* of the Lovejoy school of criticism. Condoned "in unmistakable terms" is the judgment of Irving Ribner, "The Political Problem in Shakespeare's Lancastrian Tetralogy," *Studies in Philology*, XLIX (1952), 183.

27: *P. 54.* Lily B. Campbell, *Shakespeare's Histories: Mirrors of Elizabethan Policy* (San Marino, California, 1947), pp. 273–275.

28: *P. 56.* Holinshed, *Henry IV*, p. 104.

29: *P. 57.* I am skeptical of the notion that Elizabeth was fearful of the comparison between herself and Richard II. I believe that it would have required little intuition on Shakespeare's part to guess that his queen suffered greater pangs of guilt over the execution of her cousin of Scotland than of fear at the thought of deposition by Essex or any other living man. Shakespeare, a

Londoner daily consorting with Londoners, not with Whitehall peers, could have foretold that the first impulse of London tradesmen and householders when invited to join Essex's uprising on that fateful morning of 1601 would have been to go indoors and bar the shutters.

I make the alternative suggestion then that Elizabeth's supposed distaste for being likened to Richard was an official fiction rumored by an administration that had had concrete experience with something far more ticklish in the past, her vindictive guilt at requiring them to serve as Exton to her Bolingbroke in the assassination of Mary. This is what "Richard" meant to her. As Conyers Read has written, Elizabeth [like Alexander?] was apparently "berserk" during those tense times when even Burghley was in temporary disgrace. A chain of conjecture to which I for one would lend a willing ear would be one that would include Southampton, ward in the Burghley household at the time, and also Essex, who began his political career by "pressing hard" for the exoneration of the disgraced secretary Davison, "chief scapegoat" in the whole affair (*Lord Burghley and Queen Elizabeth*, New York, 1960, pp. 378, 466, 376).

To sum up, the rumor "another Richard" permitted the authorities to harry sedition to their hearts' content (or so it would seem to authors) whereas the immensely more complicated business of "another Bolingbroke" was something they could do nothing about but hope it would not be recalled. The queen had had many a Gower to laud the assassination (see the Holinshed quotation, p. 56), and Shakespeare's surmise that this very praise would be the most galling to her conscience is only further testimony to his knowledge of the workings of the human heart.

30: ***P. 57.*** Harold Grier McCurdy's advice in connection with the violence in *Henry V* (*The Personality of Shakespeare. A Venture in Psychological Method,* New Haven, 1953, p. 83) that we look into ourselves to discover why it is that we find such behavior repulsive would be well taken if Shakespeare were writing the play McCurdy thought he was writing.

31: ***P. 58.*** Holinshed, *Henry V*, p. 42.

32: ***P. 58.*** I do not wish to associate Shakespeare with anticlericalism in any form. The portrait of Carlisle in *Richard II* shows that he was quite able to distinguish between a Bishop of London and a representative of the Establishment. See Ernest Kuhl's surmises about the position the bishop found himself in in 1599–1600, when he was made personally responsible by the newly "centralized" administration for suppressing the contemporary "libels" circulating London ("The Stationer's Company and Censorship [1599–1600]," *Library,* Series 4, IX [1929], 393).

33: ***P. 58.*** Passage after passage in the plays testifies to the value Shakespeare placed on horsemanship, almost to him a mark of nobility of character. The witching carriage described by

Vernon in *1 Henry IV* cannot have become the ploughboy leap-frogging of the wooing scene without intent.

34: ***P. 60.*** *A New Variorum Edition of 1 Henry IV,* ed. Samuel B. Hemingway (Philadelphia, 1936), p. 460. The second of the passages is by Victor Hugo.

2 HENRY IV
The Debt Prince Hal Never Promised

What sort of ideal monarch was in the making in Shakespeare's Prince Hal when events alluded to in the previous chapter broke in and caused the playwright to direct his energies into satire? The answer is plain, a prince who already had upon him the marks of the hugely politic. The effort of this present chapter will be to trace the progress of such a prince—some have called it his education—a prince not immaculately conceived but rooted in native soil and by no means even wiped clean of the stains of folklore.

I find it hard to believe that the writer who demanded for himself the recognition "I am that I am" and said of those who reckon up his abuses:

> I may be straight though they themselves be bevel

that this writer, when given a free hand to picture the education of a prince, should think of no better model of behavior than one cut out for him in Renaissance handbooks of conduct. Yet with few exceptions, a Johnson or a Goddard, this is the most that is ever required of him.[1] In one of those dawns in which it is supposed to have been bliss to be alive, the master spirit of the age forgot to tell us anything of the charms and the worth of self-determination.

The *First Part of King Henry the Fourth* gives us the education of not one, but two young men, equal in almost all respects except temperament and luck. Their education was influenced largely by the ways in which their fathers and kinsmen intended to make use of them. Hotspur, younger in political sophistication than Hal, broke the bonds of a deceitful past in one mighty scene of rage but immediately retied them. Hal was luckier; he was allowed two plays in which to untie his, and he was aided by a temperament that found more relief in the fumosity of wine than that of anger—"What, drunk with choler!" Hotspur's father exclaimed to his son. It would have been better had it been wine. The god Bacchus is a good ally against fathers.

The "Drawer Scene" (Act II, Scene iv) shows us part of Hal's education. I do not refer to an education in democracy, though that was important for him. I refer to the implications of a passage that carries all the marks of incipient *Liber*ation (if one will forgive the old Latin pun). Traditionally, not much sense has been made of the passage, it being taken for a bit of topical nonsense and mystification, beginning with Hal's sudden anger at the absent vintner, master of the humble fellow serving him wine. "Leathern-jerkin, crystal-button, knot-pated, agate-ring, puke-stocking, caddis-garter, smooth-tongue, Spanish-pouch"—it is this string of Rabelaisian epithets directed against middle-class respectability that directs *our* minds to his own predicament, that of one day having to serve this respectability. To please such as the vintner, his father had "stolen all courtesy from heaven":

> And dress'd myself in such humility
> That I did pluck allegiance from men's hearts.
> (III, ii, 50–52)

Hal would give "a thousand pounds" to break his own indenture as heir apparent and show as clean a pair of heels as Francis the drawer might for a mere pennyworth of sugar. Naturally that particular mode of escape is denied him.

There are times in a Shakespearean play when we are hard put to say what is "on" a character's mind; a case in point is Prospero's terminating the magic masque in *The Tempest.* "Never till this day/Saw I him touch'd with anger so distemper'd," said Miranda, and his anger does seem disproportionate to the occasion. For Hal, I think I have provided occasion enough. The whole, to my mind, is a particularly good example of what John Danby meant when he observed that in his histories Shakespeare had discovered an ideal medium for suggesting "growth, the dynamic of ideas passing into and out of people's minds." [2]

To the old script of the Prodigal Son, Shakespeare has added lines that bespeak a prodigal whose deepest impulse is to stay away from home, *not* to be reconciled to his father if reconciliation means submission. Prince Hal must not become a "Lancastrian," yet obviously he must grow up.[3]

2

It is perfectly clear that Shakespeare meant the education of Prince Hal to be conducted as far from his father and his dynastic troubles and perplexities as possible. With the sole exception of the battle of Shrewsbury, which it is fair to say that Hal won for his father, the Prince of Wales is absent for stage purposes from every one of his father's hours of need, not to mention his eventual hour of triumph. The only enemy of his father who ever became his own enemy was Hotspur, and he only for reasons of chivalry.

Here, from the last act of *Richard II,* is the first report a Shakespearean audience receives of the young man, a report occurring in suspicious proximity to a scene in which the recently crowned usurper, Bolingbroke, now Henry IV, is confronted with evidence of the first rebellion against him, the first of many, be it said. The speaker is Hotspur, here called Percy:

> My lord, some two days since I saw the prince,
> And told him of these triumphs held at Oxford.
> BOLINGBROKE. And what said the gallant?
> H. PERCY. His answer was: he would unto the stews,

And from the common'st creature pluck a glove,
And wear it as a favour; and with that
He would unhorse the lustiest challenger.

BOLINGBROKE. As dissolute as desperate; yet, through both,
I see some sparkles of a better hope,
Which elder days may happily bring forth.
But who comes here?

(V, iii, 13–23)

The entrant is the King's cousin Aumerle, in mad haste to report his own part in a plot that his father York has only just discovered; the father is hot behind him, and the Duchess mother behind them both, having succeeded in getting her son onto horse before the Duke. Can we mistake the comic tenor of the scene that follows, all three of them on their knees before the new King, speaking in rhyming couplets, the Duchess vowing never to rise until her son is pardoned, the Duke as fervent that "the serpent" be condemned? Aumerle is pardoned, good! But how brightly the damnable, gay insouciance of the absent Prince and heir apparent shines, set off against the unlovely complexities revealed in these lines to York:

BOLINGBROKE. O heinous, strong, and bold conspiracy!
O loyal father of a treacherous son!

Thou sheer, immaculate, and silver fountain,
From whence this stream through muddy passages
Hath held his current and defil'd himself!
Thy overflow of good converts to bad,
And thy abundant goodness shall excuse
This deadly blot in thy digressing son.

(*Ibid.*, 59–66)

The whole episode, including York's response to the above, touched with unmistakable mercantile overtones—". . . thriftless sons [spending] their scraping fathers' gold./Mine honour lives when his dishonour dies"—will, though only in retrospect, provide commentary on the uneasy relations holding between royal father and son in the next play. As for "muddy passages," the King is beset with them to the end of his days, how beset only the reader who delves into his Holinshed knows.[4] On the last of them, still unattended by his son, he receives news of the crushing of the final rebellion and shortly thereafter suffers an apoplectic stroke. Here he is inquiring after his son just before the reception of the news:

K. HENRY. Why art thou not at Windsor with him, Thomas?
CLARENCE. He is not there to-day; he dines in London.
K. HENRY. And how accompanied? canst thou tell that?

CLARENCE. With Poins and other his continual followers.
K. HENRY. Most subject is the fattest soil to weeds;
And he, the noble image of my youth,
Is overspread with them . . .

(*2 Henry IV*, IV, iv, 50–56)

To ask what grounds there are for this king's still holding to the belief that his son is an image of his own dedicated youth is to inquire into one of the oddities of human nature. The hoary assumption of the preceding generation that their offspring *are* themselves, reborn and ready for a fresh start, explains completely both the recurring need for revolt and the peculiar difficulties for the children of effecting it.

Let us go directly to the scene in *1 Henry IV* where it is thought by so many that Bolingbroke once and for all, and rather easily it must be said, succeeded in making his son over into an image of himself. It is of course the pivotal scene in any representation of the reform of Prince Hal.

The traditional interpretation of the scene (Act III, Scene ii), which I shall call the Audience Scene, takes one of two forms: either that the heir apparent finally reconciles himself to the inevitable when he meets with his father, and then and there undertakes to reform as he said he would on his first appearance in the play; or that his eventual reform has been something that he had carefully planned, even to the extent of foreseeing the occasion, and this is the occasion. What, one asks, could be plainer? To dispute such readings must seem unnecessarily captious in view of the hundreds of performances founded on one or the other of these interpretations and undoubtedly making for a coherent and exciting play. If I dispute them, as I propose to do, it is not because they are insufficiently exciting or insufficiently historical and true to life, but solely because they are not the readings that come out of the text. To read the Audience Scene as an element in the play with more of a central function than merely confirming the promises made in the Soliloquy (Act I, Scene ii), will be to depart very far from the traditional interpretation.

Shakespeare gives us a Prince who had no intention of reforming when he went into conference with his father, who resisted his father throughout three-quarters of the interview,[5] and who was tricked into premature and emotional declaration toward the end of it only by his father's last resort—that of calling him a coward and a traitor. (The latter word, when used against Mortimer, had turned Hotspur into a traitor.)

This is not only the reading that best squares with the text, bringing to life the Soliloquy as no other reading that I know of does, but it happens also to be the one that soonest calls to mind, albeit ironically, the equivalent scene from the old but still popular "Queens" play, the anonymous *Famous Victories of Henry the*

Fifth that supplied Shakespeare with so many cues for the pranks and tavern matter of his own play. Like most folklore, *Famous Victories* is characterized through and through by sensationalism, which is the last thing that can be said of Shakespeare's father-son interview—except for its ending. By supplying a ternary movement throughout, Shakespeare did succeed in making at least the ending of his long, unrelieved near-monologue properly sensational:

> Three times he did his son beseech,
> Adown the tearis ran,
> But when the prince his father left,
> He was a changed man.

Here we have the very substance of the Audience Scene as it might conceivably have appeared in ballad form. However much unlike the two plays, *Famous Victories* and *1 Henry IV*, are in all other respects, they are alike in having the reform of Hal both sudden and sensational, if not complete.[6]

Before examining in detail the extended ordeal to which Shakespeare subjected his Prince—an ordeal that was no ordeal according to the traditional view, since the Prince clearly foresaw it all—I should like to pose three sets of related questions:

First, does the Audience Scene represent the Prince's own

chosen moment for announcing his reform? If it does *not*, and if in reality he let slip the initiative to his father, of what use is the impression lodged earlier, that of the young calculator whose sole professed purpose was to gain credit for a reformation to himself and to himself alone? Could he have been that unwatchful of his interests?

Second, if it *is* the moment he had long anticipated (and no one has ever suggested that the battlefield of Shrewsbury was not stage enough!), why did he give such a poor account of himself when it arrived, letting things go so far as to hear himself berated as a coward and a traitor? Why did the interview take so long? Above all, why was it private?

Third, why, after the interview and on his return to the tavern, did Shakespeare put into the Prince's mouth the only lines in either play in which he openly invites Falstaff's impudent suggestions instead of, as elsewhere, turning them to ridicule?

> PRINCE. I am good friends with my father and may do anything.
>
> FALSTAFF. Rob me the exchequer the first thing thou dost, and do it with unwashed hands too.
>
> (III, iii, 202–205)

These are questions that one has a right to expect any director to ask himself who has the responsibility of staging a coherent production of *1 Henry IV*. How would he pace the scene, how instruct the actor who must listen to one hundred and ten lines of verse before he delivers his answer, a premeditated one, according to the conventional view?

There are, of course, corollaries to the above questions, which it would be well to anticipate before they arise. If Shakespeare intended the Prince's early statement of purpose (the first-act Soliloquy) to provide a complete explanation of all subsequent events in the play, then obviously he should have written a different Audience Scene or perhaps none at all. Something possibly sudden and sensational, but above all *public,* was demanded. It would be easily in the grasp of the writer who penned the lyric Vernon speech, of which one is so justly fond, a speech delivered in the enemy camp by an enemy and therefore providing as objective proof of the Prince's accession to chivalry as need be devised. To say that Shakespeare's public expected an Audience Scene from recollection of previous dramatizations of the tale is only to raise the question of why he did not meet their expectation more fully. If for some reason he did not want a public confrontation of father and son in full view of respective retinues[7]—grievances stated, fears allayed, promises made—then he could have arranged a private one, one in keeping with the "blushing citals" subsequently made on the battlefield. In such an interview, the Prince would have confessed that which would have surprised no one, because it might be partly true—that he had been consorting with low company so as to become better acquainted with his future subjects—the view that best served history and the one proposed by Warwick toward the end of *2 Henry IV* when the Prince's behavior was still felt by the court to be problematical.

Secondly, if Shakespeare intended the Audience Scene to represent the great moment anticipated by the Soliloquy, then he dangerously trifled with us in that comic scene of role-playing between Hal and Falstaff the night before. Without it, and it was not called for by his model (the role-playing in *Famous Victories* involved Hal and the Lord Chief Justice and with quite different effect), there was sufficient incidental comedy to put us in a proper frame of mind to expect a changed Prince the following morning. I refer to the mimicking of Hotspur, the relaxed joking about his terrible reputation for fighting, all in the good tradition of the hero-athlete who cannot be bothered to train. We expect such a hero to win, for he has what it takes.

Altogether different is the role-playing with Falstaff, a rehearsal of the coming event at court conducted in a frame of mind so frivolous, so completely wide of the mark that it can only strike one in retrospect as utterly irrelevant.[8] Anyone with an interest or stake in the dynastic issue who might overhear both of these, the promises made in the Soliloquy and the mock rehearsal of their fulfillment, the two so widely separated in stage time, could scarcely be blamed if he took the second of the two as representing the true state of affairs in the realm—and ominous indeed for the fortunes of the King. We, of course, as spectators of the drama, are very much in that position.

We may now attend to the Audience Scene. After clearing the council chamber, the King begins, as expected, with a description of his son's way of life, "Such poor, such bare, such lewd, such mean attempts," prefaced, however, with notice that he accepts the same as punishment from heaven for his own past "mistreading." Even without our knowledge of the recent uproarious scene of "banishment," the relentless pressure with which the King proceeds to press the attack suggests a son who is not listening very hard, if indeed he is listening at all; he has come to the interview with "his blood inclin'd to mirth." [9] To the first of the typical paternal reproaches, he answers mechanically that the whole thing has been greatly exaggerated. He lays what small justice there is in the "slanders" [10] to his youth and offers his respectful submission.

> . . . for some things true, wherein my youth
> Hath faulty wandr'd and irregular,
> Find pardon on my true submission.
>
> (III, ii, 26–28)

To let oneself be impressed by the "manly" forthrightness of the Prince at this juncture is to miss the point entirely. Since the world began, youth has thought it knew the right things to say to mollify its elders. This King is not impressed—nor should we be. Can he sincerely be blaming his "youth," this young Prince who sent the sheriff packing the night before with such easy authority? He would despise himself if he meant it.[11]

The King is not satisfied, and why should he be? He breaks in, "God pardon thee . . ." had I conducted myself at your age as you are now doing. It is the time-honored reproach of age to wayward youth and, alas, falls on unheeding ears. But now we should take note of a trait that may luckily not be common to all fathers. The King weeps. The father, who had publicly declared in the opening scene of the play that he wished the Prince were another's son, now weeps because, forsooth, he has seen so little of him!

It is about time that someone took proper note of the marked histrionic side of Henry Bolingbroke. Read his tearful complaining to the Prince on his deathbed at the end of Part II, and ask wherein he differs from the self-pitying Richard he treated so coldly when he was in the position of dictating terms, not lamenting them (*Richard II*, IV, i, 268 ff.). In this department, Shakespeare's Bolingbroke is the Henry of the crude *Famous Victories*. Here is a play that Shakespeare probably saw acted, for the day is past when it was proposed that he had a hand in it. In the parallel scene of *Famous Victories*, the king father speaks two short verse paragraphs of self-commiseration, both followed by stage directions, "The King weeps"; and the son, who had come swaggering into the chamber displaying a dagger, falls into abject surrender and self-reproach:

> My conscience accuseth me, most soueraign Lord, and welbeloued father, to answere. . . . but farre be the thoughts of any such pretended mischiefe: and I most humbly render it to your Maiesties hand . . . those wilde & reprobate company I abandon, & vtterly abolish their company for euer. . . . Pardon me, sweet father, pardon me: good my Lord of Exeter speak for me: pardon me, pardon good father, not a word: ah he will not speak a word: A Harry, now thrice vnhappie Harry. But what shal I do? I wil go take me into some solitarie place, and there lament my sinfull life, and when I haue done, I wil laie me downe and die.[12]

A reference by the father in the next scene to the "lesson" he had given his son may be justified, but it would be calculated to make a brother playwright wince. Shakespeare, in his father-son confrontation, amended matters. The response of Hal to Bolingbroke's tears is a cold and embarrassed:

I shall hereafter, my thrice-gracious lord,
Be more myself.

The King sees he has made no impression.[13] There is a third and final assault on his son, and as everybody knows, it succeeds. The rush of words, so reminiscent of Hotspur smarting under the indignities put upon him by this same "vile politician Bolingbroke," is Shakespeare's way of telling us that another scion of chivalry has been used by a cleverer man (not that it was not a close thing):

Do not think so; you shall not find it so:
And God forgive them, that so much have sway'd
Your majesty's good thoughts away from me!
I will redeem all this on Percy's head,
And in the closing of some glorious day . . .
(III, ii, 129–133)

and high time too, for there is nothing tragic in the peripety of the man who speaks here. They are the first serious words we have heard from him in the play. Manipulated he may have been by a cleverer man than himself, but the justifying end was history:

K. HENRY. Percy, Northumberland,
The Archbishop's Grace of York, Douglas, Mortimer,
Capitulate against us and are up.

(*Ibid.*, 118–120)

In what other play has a dramatist so loaded the odds against his hero and left him so little time to spare? (It is no accident that Shakespeare moved the father-son interview back *before* the battle of Shrewsbury, though his Holinshed told him it took place afterward.) In contrast to the gathering rebel forces, the King's support is all but unnamed until the very eve of battle. If the scene we have just reviewed, besides being the most eagerly awaited, also turns out to be the longest, there is good reason for it. Shakespeare has at one and the same time done full justice to "history," to folklore, and to a hidden drama of Morality, though not, I think, to the morality generally supposed.

3

If the foregoing is to gain acceptance (if it is not premature to conceive of such currents flowing under the surface of a plain Anglo-Saxon play) something must be done about the Soliloquy, a part of the play that would seem to many to conflict uncomfortably with what I have so far set forth. The Soliloquy unquestionably requires a word before we can move forward with the Prodigal through the remaining scenes of his stage life.

We shall see comparatively little of him after his interview with his father, and he will be but superficially changed. Only when he appears crowned and in royal regalia shall we be certain that all is well. These things have been known and have been commented on. How is it that the Soliloquy has provoked so little curiosity? Probably because soliloquies are generally held to have performed a very simple range of function in the old plays in which they were used. I give Prince Hal's in its entirety:

> I know you all, and will awhile uphold
> The unyok'd humour of your idleness:
> Yet herein will I imitate the sun,
> Who doth permit the base contagious clouds
> To smother up his beauty from the world,
> That when he please again to be himself,
> Being wanted, he may be more wonder'd at,
> By breaking through the foul and ugly mists
> Of vapours that did seem to strangle him.
> If all the year were playing holidays,
> To sport would be as tedious as to work;
> But when they seldom come, they wish'd for come,
> And nothing pleaseth but rare accidents.

So, when this loose behaviour I throw off,
And pay the debt I never promised,
By how much better than my word I am
By so much shall I falsify men's hopes;
And like bright metal on a sullen ground,
My reformation, glittering o'er my fault,
Shall show more goodly and attract more eyes
Than that which hath no foil to set it off.
I'll so offend to make offence a skill;
Redeeming time when men think least I will.

(I, ii, 217–239)

Here, then, is the well-known Soliloquy that constitutes the primary evidence for Prince Hal's inherited Machiavellianism, the secondary being his rejection of Falstaff. Bearing in mind an unanswered question—why did the Prince not make better use of his opportunity when it presented itself two mornings later?—I propose to examine the incriminating document somewhat more closely than I think it has been in the past.

The Soliloquy is two things, a formal dramaturgic device and a revelation of what is going on deep in the womb of this most interesting of plays. For the first, it was a bold stroke of Shakespeare's to commence his play with two long scenes evenly divided between the serious and the comic. Although a London audience at this time might be expected to recognize in Prince Hal a folk hero about to launch into another cycle of riot and reform,[14] still, with a play like *Famous Victories* fairly fresh in their minds, they might be supposed to have been unprepared for a King Henry with quite such serious matters on his hands and for a Prince Hal who is proving quite such an inconvenience to him. The Soliloquy told them that their playwright knew what he was about.

Far more important, however, than the promise of reform, for which the Soliloquy provided formal assurance, is the question of the time and the manner. This new play makes that much clear from the start. As will be seen, Shakespeare had his own ideas on the subject, differing, too, from most of the ideas that have been attributed to him.

The Soliloquy conveys the impression of a young man seeking a way out of his difficulties by having his cake and eating it too, the cake entailing notions that might possibly not have occurred to a Puritanically minded audience, much less to a Bolingbroke father. To understand this, we must turn to Shakespeare's own Sonnet 52, to lines that have long been credited with supplying the central imagery both of Soliloquy and of Audience Scene. It is not the mere fact that one of his own sonnets is, so to speak, quoted, but that it is a very particular sonnet that is quoted that should claim our attention. The near-unconscious finesse of the thing may one day be recognized along with other Shakespearean attributes as typically Shakespearean.

The sonnet is about holidays and holiday feasting. It is maintained that their best enjoyment, as with the poet's own feasts of love, lies in their necessary infrequency. Like the bright holiday garments donned to make "some special instant special blest," so does one's love—if one has the "blessed key" to the wardrobe—make one feel but the richer for its "seldom pleasure" that is "so solemn and so rare." This thought underlies the King's argument to his son in the Audience Scene:

> Thus did I keep my person fresh and new;
> My presence, like a robe pontifical,
> Ne'er seen but wonder'd at: and so my state,
> Seldom but sumptuous, showed like a feast,
> And won by rareness such solemnity.
>
> (III, ii, 55–59)

Apparently, if love can be associated with holidays, so can Majesty. The show of Majesty, if used sparingly, has a certain "potential."

This is the last thing that Shakespeare meant in his sonnet or in any play or sonnet that he ever penned.

For thy sweet love remember'd such wealth brings
That then I scorn to change my state with kings.

To arrange to have one's thoughts come so patly to the lips of a king, and a Machiavellian one at that, is surely the privilege of a dramatist who ranges far afield, and in his ranging strikes at the central dilemma of Rule—power divorced from love. Read the progress of this king through the two parts of the play right to to his deathbed—see page 109 and note—and you will find yourself reading Dantean comedy.

Fortunately, no more than Shakespeare does this Prince have in mind such parsimonious doling out of his presence, as we know from having heard his Soliloquy. If, to convince himself of his good intentions, he also "quoted" the sonnet, it is because he had heard it so often, and will yet again in the coming interview. He is simply using such royal thoughts as are available to him. That they represent an obvious subversion of his author's original sonnet he is not in a position to know. All unconsciously he makes his own correction; Shakespeare sees to that. It is institutionalized sentiment that we hear from him as he steps forward on the empty stage to tell us what, as he supposed, was really on his mind. Holidays are not for every day, and some day I mean to go to work. It is simple enough, and he thinks he means what he says. But, as everyone must have seen, the words do not come out right.

Or rather they *do* come out right, for himself and his future subjects,[15] for whether he knows it or not, doled-out parsimonious *agape*, kingly love, is not what he has in him to give.

The cross-purposes with his father show most clearly, of course, in the sun imagery that they both employ, the imagery that had been Shakespeare's chief stock-in-trade since he began this sequence of plays with *Richard II*. The son believes that if he is at fault it is for letting "base contagious clouds to smother up his beauty from the world," the father that he has shone too much—that he has spent himself, that the world is weary of his sight. Obviously, the son does not agree, not holding with his father, or with Richard before his father, that the mere inoperative presence of Majesty is something necessarily sunlike, or that when it is, it can be diminished by use. Majesty, like chivalry, is a quality of action. The suspicion grows upon us that, whether he knows it or not, this Prince intends a rule in which perhaps every day *is* holiday.

How drab the thought now that in his Soliloquy he is only announcing his intention of one day rolling up his sleeves and going to work.[16] This is no more than his father was asking of him, probably no more than the spectators of the play would ask. They are told something quite different. When, in a somewhat disconnected line of thought, the image of holiday trappings merges with the dominant sun imagery, any notion that the former will "be so solemn and so rare" is rather lost from view. Work lightened by love, work made holiday by confraternity—the excitement of it is in the Crispin speech—this constitutes the debt the ruler owes his subjects. It is the glorious spending of the sonnets. The expression may not be of the clearest, having been borrowed from others, his father and Shakespeare, but it *is* clear that the Prince has glimpsed a way out of the toils of everlasting respectability, of everlasting Lancaster "policy." No doubt of it, if Shakespeare had succeeded in writing a play about the ideal monarch—Cordelia represents the closest he got to it—there would be much sonnet "matter" in that play, the "hugely politic" somehow contained in "mutual render, only me for thee." At any rate, I should like it conceded that the Soliloquy carries as much or more explanation of the Drawer Scene previously considered than of the subsequent Audience Scene.

It is hardly accidental that both father and son make promises to be "more like themselves" within twenty-one lines of each other in the text. The Prince's place on the stage at the conclusion of his Soliloquy is taken by King and court to discuss unfinished business begun back in the opening scene of the play. Machiavellianism unfolds on the spot where moments before we had heard the young man say he would make a "skill" of behavior offensive to his father and would cease doing so when he chose. Now, in even fewer moments, Bolingbroke accomplishes what he had skillfully been plotting when we first saw him—pretending to be earnest about a crusade that he had already put from his mind, pretending disappointment, establishing his fair-mindedness by praising young Percy and wishing his kind for a son, pretending to be too angry to discuss "this young Percy's pride," and now, where Hal had but recently been standing, provoking a quarrel with the Percy family that will be final and irremediable.

> I will from henceforth rather be myself,
> Mighty, and to be fear'd, than my condition,
> Which hath been smooth as oil, soft as young down . . .
> (I, iii, 5–7)

Beside such hoary Machiavellianism the efforts of the Prince in the like direction appear positively idealistic. And probably at bottom they are. Though he may not know it, he has been using his shabby associates as untold generations have before and since, as a means of attacking the values of the generation presuming to bring them up, educate them. Now, of course, he has been used himself. That is the Shakespearean humor of the thing: the User Used.

The genuine drama of the Audience Scene totally conceals the fact that the success of the King has consisted largely in his having got his son to talk like Hotspur, that "Mars in swathling clothes, this infant warrior" (to repeat a bit of the rhetoric we have heard). Any such eventuality must have been far from the young man's mind back at the Boar's Head when he was parodying that same "Hotspur of the North"—"he that kills me some six or seven dozen of Scots at a breakfast, washes his hands, and says to his wife, 'Fie upon this quiet life! I want work,' " Now it is:

> And I will die a hundred thousand deaths
> Ere break the smallest parcel of this vow.
> (III, ii, 158–159)

To which his father answers:

> A hundred thousand rebels die in this!

Here we have the same ironic work at mind that within a year or two will have that brittle hero Brutus confer "several bastardy" on "every drop of blood,/ That every Roman bears [who might] break the smallest particle/ Of any promise that hath pass'd from him." Brutus had just extracted a promise from others to assist in killing a man who, on his own admission, had done no harm. When the book about Shakespeare and The Rant is written, it is most certain to contain something about numbers. There will be cited Hamlet's invitation to heap "Millions of acres on us, till our ground,/ Singeing his pate against the burning zone/ Make Ossa like a wart!" There will be cited Prince Hal's:

> And I will die a hundred thousand deaths
> Ere break the smallest parcel of this vow.

It is a Prince possessed still of an heroic innocence who leaves the interview with his father. "I am good friends with my father, and may do anything" (he says back at the tavern). Perhaps such an innocence might not be a bad thing, thought Shakespeare, as he read his Holinshed and looked about at the contemporary scene.

4

We may now proceed to put together the remaining bits of the play and of the play following, in which, as it has been pointed out, the Prince is a relatively infrequent figure. Except for some brief and honest heroics on the field of Shrewsbury, he is largely involved in comedy right up to the end of Part I.[17] The comedy is often of an equivocal nature, as if the author could not bring himself to let his youth be identified with the successful Lancastrian cause. I shall describe one scene, the last in the play, before going on to Part II, where everything is changed. There we see the Prince as it were awaiting his father's death and his own accession to the throne. The scene I shall select to describe in that play is usually considered to be of small consequence. Thereupon we shall go directly to the King's deathbed and to the coronation, the latter inevitably entailing the rejection of Falstaff.

On the field of Shrewsbury we see Hal for the last time in public, whether court or battlefield, until he himself is king. The heroic innocence that I have mentioned is with him to the last—maintained not entirely without Shakespeare's help. Prince John has fought well, and Hal has as it were forgiven him for having supplanted him at the council table:

> [*Exeunt* JOHN OF LANCASTER *and* WESTMORELAND.
> PRINCE. By God, thou hast deceiv'd me, Lancaster;
> I did not think thee lord of such a spirit:
> Before, I lov'd thee as a brother, John;
> But now, I do respect thee as my soul.
>
> (V, iv, 17–20)

The Prince asks of his father and is given permission to dispose of the captured Douglas. He generously cedes the honor to his brother. (There is no precedent in Holinshed for this, Holinshed simply recording, ". . . and for his valiantnesse, of the king [Douglas was] frankelie and freelie delivered" [18]):

> Then, brother John of Lancaster, to you
> This honorable bounty shall belong.
> Go to the Douglas, and deliver him
> Up to his pleasure, ransomless, and free:
> His valour shown upon our crests to-day
> Hath taught us how to cherish such high deeds,
> Even in the bosom of our adversaries.
> (V, v, 25–31)

The answer of Prince John is like nothing recorded in chivalric literature, though the cheating of Glaucus by Diomedes in the *Iliad*—a fair exchange of gifts that was not fair—may belong in the same category of humor:

> I thank your Grace for this high courtesy,
> Which I shall give away immediately.

No, Prince John is not very good at this sort of thing. A short speech by the King, giving directions for the morrow, and the play is over. If many a reader has missed this bit of byplay, and play producers have not known what to do with it, they have had good reason. It was omitted from the First Folio by Shakespeare's own good friends and literary executors.[19] If it had not survived in quarto, we should be none the wiser. Is it an instance of

"Truth's a dog must to kennel; he must be whipped out, when my Lady Brach may stand by th' fire and stink"? Hardly. The comedies are full of such places that almost proclaim themselves "topical," some tingling with a gesture and motion that are no longer there. To retain such a mute bit of farce, such a complicated historical "joke" as the above could hardly be justified by the knowing editor. Quite possibly it was written to be included in the quarto.

5

The Second Part of King Henry the Fourth is well advanced before we see Prince Hal once more, and it is in low times oppressed with injustice and sickness. The scene is Eastcheap, the Boar's Head Tavern, whither the Prince arrives for the last time, unaccountably weary—some have thought from being long in the saddle:

> PRINCE. Before God, I am exceeding weary.
>
> POINS. Is it come to that? I had thought weariness durst not have attached one of so high blood.
>
> (II, ii, 1–4)

But joking does not suit the Prince's present mood. What follows is—rather could be—the counterpart of the moving talk of Hamlet and Horatio in the third act of *Hamlet*. Hal needs someone whom he could call his "soul's election," needs to evoke from someone the response, "O, my dear lord!" Instead he sees in the cynical shallowness of the youth who is supposed to be his twin (by "the weight of a hair," said Falstaff, II, iv, 276–277) the frightful possibility that he is worse, his alter ego. "What a disgrace is it to me to remember thy name, or to know thy face tomorrow! or to take note how many pair of silk stockings thou hast." But Poins does not even recognize that there is more than chaffing going on here. In turning the joke, he shows the basic conventionality that informs his character; he has recourse to easy morality:

> How ill it follows, after you have laboured so hard you should talk so idly! Tell me, how many good young princes would do so, their fathers being so sick as yours at this time is?
>
> (II, ii, 32–36)

Here is the place decisively to locate the Prince's reform, if we must locate it, not the spurious reform of the Audience Scene, but a reform self-induced, self-initiated. To be taught morality by a Poins! A man who sees so clearly what he has done to himself, what channels of feeling he has come close to cutting himself off from, is one who is already on the road to better things.

Marry, I tell thee, it is not meet that I should be sad, now my father is sick: albeit I could tell to thee,—as to one it pleases me, for fault of a better, to call my friend,—I could be sad, and sad indeed too.

. . . let the end try the man.

But I tell thee my heart bleeds inwardly that my father is so sick; and keeping such vile company as thou art hath in reason taken from me all ostentation of sorrow.

POINS. The reason?

PRINCE. What wouldst thou think of me, if I should weep?

POINS. I would think thee a most princely hypocrite.

PRINCE. It would be every man's thought; and thou art a blessed fellow to think as every man thinks: never a man's thought in the world keeps the road-way better than thine: every man would think me a hypocrite indeed.

(*Ibid.*, 44–66)

After this the Prince participates in some tavern comedy as of old, Falstaff, drawers, and all, but it is lifeless compared with the former high spirits and camaraderie. Poins disappears from the play thereafter—though it is rumored that the Prince has been seen with him. We do not see the Prince again for two full Shakespearean acts.

In Act IV the King is lying dying at Westminster. Let each one choose for himself the stage directions that should accompany the Prince's entrance:

> PRINCE. Who saw the Duke of Clarence?
> CLARENCE. I am here, brother, full of heaviness.
> PRINCE. How now! rain within doors, and none abroad!
> How doth the king?
> GLOUCESTER. Exceeding ill.
> PRINCE. Heard he the good news yet?
> Tell it him.
> GLOUCESTER. He alter'd much upon the hearing it.
> PRINCE. If he be sick with joy, he will recover
> without physic.
> WARWICK. Not so much noise, my lords. Sweet
> prince, speak low:
> The king your father is dispos'd to sleep.
>
> (IV, v, 7–16)

But then the contrast when the Prince is alone, the contrast we have grown to expect! Sitting by his father and mistaking his deep sleep for death:

> My gracious lord! my father!
> This sleep is sound indeed; this is a sleep

That from this golden rigol hath divorc'd
So many English kings. Thy due from me
Is tears and heavy sorrows of the blood,
Which nature, love, and filial tenderness
Shall, O dear father! pay thee plenteously:
My due from thee is this imperial crown,
Which, as immediate from thy place and blood,
Derives itself to me. Lo! here it sits.

(*Ibid.*, 33–42)

No hearers on this occasion, no expectation or likelihood of report or public rumor, only the whispered "me for thee." Could there be conceived a better answer to the absent Poins? [20]

The scene is actually but a preliminary, for the reconciliation demanded by legend must follow; there must be an awakening of the King, a missing of the borrowed crown, expression of hurt feelings, and explanation. Though the mistake was made in no spirit of avaricious haste, the King must be convinced of that as well as the audience. As usual, we cannot say enough for the art that rises to this occasion, the Shakespearean art. Where did it come from, this cry of the King, after forty lines of histrionics and self-pity, the one cry that could bind father and son together and give them momentary understanding?

O my poor kingdom! sick with civil blows.
When that my care could not withhold thy riots,
What wilt thou do when riot is thy care?
O! thou wilt be a wilderness again,
Peopled with wolves, thy old inhabitants.

(*Ibid.*, 132–136)

Can we doubt that it is the first expression of truly royal concern that the heir apparent and king-to-be has ever heard, the first statecraft that savored of something other than craft? [21] Here is the answer:

O! pardon me, my liege; but for my tears,
The moist impediments unto my speech,
I had forstall'd this dear and deep rebuke
Ere you with grief had spoke and I had heard
The course of it so far. Here is your crown;
And he that wears the crown immortally
Long guard it yours!

(*Ibid.*, 137–143)

The answer is of equal length with the King's charge, both too long to give in full, but anyone following the argument may wish to read the full text for himself. We have heard the Prince on the defensive before and have known what to think of it. Here on the eve of his demonstration to the world of just "how much better than my word" he was, the words ring differently, the opposite now of facile temporizing, rather of urgency, a fear of having carried things too far and perhaps already being too late. *Will* he now be understood? [22]

> . . . if I do feign,
> O! let me in my present wildness die
> And never live to show the incredulous world
> The noble change that I have purposed.
> (*Ibid.*, 150–153)

6

The new King is absolutely obliged to get rid of Falstaff. In blaming him for it, we are blaming Shakespeare for endowing a minor character in his plot with so much life, but to give him that life was essential to the working out of the theme. We become involved in the same dilemma in which Shakespeare seems to have been involved. In any case, it is perfectly clear that it is Shakespeare himself, not the hapless Hal, who was working toward the dismissal of Falstaff from the start of Part II, the first step being to give him into the company of Prince John. Though he considers him a cold fish and no fit company for a drinking man, still under Prince John this Lord of Misrule, this Absolute of Saturnalia, is as happy on the side of law and order as he had been stealing purses with Hal. (If he has the pox, that is another matter.) He has exchanged body-stealing for purse-stealing as the current poor abuse of the time. Perhaps, indeed, he is happier, because now he commands respect, and Falstaff thrives on respect. True, Falstaff loved Hal and misses him. He says that Hal's love was worth a million pounds to him.

But granting the above, we are still inclined to say that the dismissal, when it came, should not have been so unfeeling and cold. To answer this objection, I propose to examine rapidly the whole sequence leading up to it. It may be that Shakespeare saw opportunities of humor too plainly in keeping with the serious theme of his play not to be taken advantage of. As we know, the play ends with a curtain speech by Prince John, presuming to speak for the royal pleasure at the prospect of invading France. To be so misunderstood! And yet—not entirely! Let us see if Shakespeare has not foreseen a time when princes must also pay for their follies and pay to the same extent that they had enjoyed them.

The rejection of Falstaff takes place under the eye of the Lord Chief Justice, and this perhaps is the key to the whole thing, for what Hal must live down is not so much the criminality of his former ways (though they surely bordered on the criminal) as the juvenility. The Lord Chief Justice is there expressly to help him. No doubt a good half of the audience recalled the scene of role-playing in *Famous Victories*, and half expected a return to the level of the ear-boxing of that play—"What! rate, rebuke, and roughly send to prison/ The immediate heir of England! Was this easy? May this be wash'd in Lethe, and forgotten?" (V, ii, 70–72). If so, they were disappointed. On this afternoon, Londoners saw as noble a scene of submission to appointed authority as ever graced the stage—or history—an image of themselves and possibilities of political responsibility that few of them would ever forget:

> You did commit me:
> For which, I do commit into your hand
> The unstained sword that you have us'd to bear;
> With this remembrance, that you use the same
> With the like bold, just, and impartial spirit
> As you have done 'gainst me. There is my hand:
> You shall be as father to my youth . . .
> (*Ibid.*, 112–118)

A splendid, unforgettable scene—and encouraging of more than one reflection. Who would have the temerity to tamper with such a scene? Shakespeare himself, just as he had tampered with the dignity of the closing moments of Shrewsbury.

The play is not quite over. A youth whose conduct up to this moment has hardly been cut to heroic pattern has yet to make payment in full. He wanted a public reformation, and public it will be, in full view of as many townsfolk as can be squeezed onto the stage.

Act V of the play is made up of five scenes. The first is laid in Gloucestershire; it is devoted to showing Falstaff's anticipatory relish of the pleasure his friend Hal will have from hearing accounts of what he, Falstaff, has seen of provincial corruption, the aping of what is better done at court. The next scene is that of the announcement of King Henry IV's death, complete with the gloomy fears of the Lord Chief Justice ("O, God, I fear all will be overturn'd") and almost immediate nullification of those fears by the bearing of the new ruler. Next follows a scene showing Falstaff's reception of the news during some rural merrymaking; his mounting horse and riding for London like an avenging angel ("Blessed are they that have been my friends, and woe to my Lord Chief Justice!"); a very short scene showing Falstaff's womenfolk deprived of his protection and left to the mercies of the law; and finally the scene of the coronation procession and Falstaff's dismissal. It is the last that we have been working toward.

For an explanation of the cold kingly asperity that responds to the voice from the crowd, "My king! My Jove! I speak to thee, my heart!" we need only return in mind to the thrilling scene of this Jove's submission to the principle of responsibility, mere moments away in stage time.

> KING HENRY V. You all look strangely on me: [*To the* CHIEF JUSTICE] and you most;
> You are, I think, assur'd I love you not.
>
> (V, ii, 62–63)

If ever lines bespoke unwritten stage directions, it is these lines. Hard it always is to read in the eyes of persons one is addressing the poor opinion one suspects they have of one, but for him who has just reaffirmed to his father "the noble change that I have purposed"—hard beyond hard! To read in the eyes of that father's most trusted adviser a gloomy expectation of who knows what mongrel behavior . . . ! Ah, to be so misunderstood!

On our first meeting with Hal in company with his Boar's Head cronies, he had told us plainly that he had merely "been smothering up his beauty from the world" to be the more wonder'd at when he "pleased to be himself again." He has been good to his word, he has made his submission, he has proceeded to the coronation. Suddenly, this messenger from the forsworn past joyously echoing all the insinuations and affronting hints that we have been hearing from the start of their associated careers—royal protection for highwaymen forsooth . . . !

PISTOL. The heavens thee guard and keep, most royal imp of fame!
FALSTAFF. God save thee, my sweet boy!

(V, v, 46–48)

Well, all we can say is that the young man has deserved it. He has no one to blame but himself. It is unfortunate, *most* unfortunate, but then again . . . so well earned. "Thou art mad to say it!" is Lady Macbeth's cry to the messenger who seemed to read her guilty thoughts. From Hal a wrathful tight-lipped self-control:

My lord chief justice, speak to that vain man.

Who will believe him if this is allowed to pass? Probably such things do not happen in life or in the lives of kings. It is high stage comedy.

A final word for Falstaff.[23] It must be admitted that Falstaff, unlike the messenger to Lady Macbeth, has behaved like a madman. ("Have you your wits? know you what 'tis you speak?" said the Lord Chief Justice.) The proper treatment for madmen is at least temporary confinement in the expectation of cure. It would be the height of hypocrisy on the part of the King to propose such a thing—we remember too vividly his participation in mockery of kings in days past at the Boar's Head. Banishment is the measure that befits the occasion. He was a young man when his own father was banished by Richard, for less reason too, though also "on pain of death."

> And, as we hear you do reform yourselves,
> We will, according to your strength and qualities,
> Give you advancement.
>
> (*Ibid.*, 73–75)

I find myself in disagreement with the critics who have sorrowed over this scene more than I think Falstaff himself. Falstaff expects to be sent for in private. He will learn. In the meantime, there are the reassuring words of the King's brother, John:

> LANCASTER. I like this fair proceeding of the king's.
> He hath intent his wonted followers
> Shall all be very well provided for;
> But all are banish'd till their conversations
> Appear more wise and modest to the world.

CHIEF JUSTICE. And so they are.
LANCASTER. The king hath call'd his parliament, my lord.
CHIEF JUSTICE. He hath.

(*Ibid.*, 103–110)

And then the concluding lines, "I heard a bird so sing . . ." Already the dramatist's thoughts are turning away from Falstaff to matters of more pressing concern. Some believe that the Epilogue that follows, promising more of Falstaff, is not to be attributed to Shakespeare.

7

Could Shakespeare, had he persevered, have succeeded in giving dramatic flesh to what we may imagine was his original concept? An heroic figure wielding the fullest conceivable secular power, a Tamburlaine one could live as comfortably with as one could with Hal in Eastcheap? The materials were there in Holinshed (a selection will be found in an Appendix), and you might suppose that all he had to do was write a play from them. At any rate, he did not. Instead, he resorted to the two very human instruments of burlesque and blame.[24] Perhaps it is just as well. As suggested by Bronowski, there may ultimately be no sort of compatibility between simple goodness, which we all aspire to, and power, let alone enormous power:

> In the fight against natural chaos, the guilt of society is that it is society. The guilt is order, and the guilty are those whose authority imposes order.[25]

Perhaps here was Shakespeare's real obstacle, his real antagonist —the rights of I am that I am, the rights even of Falstaff.

We cannot say. All we know for certain is that to the end of his writing career the subject kept trying his soul. We find the negative evidence in the recurrent irony at the expense of the "mystery"[26] of statecraft, the divinity that hedges kings, at least Claudiuses. We see it in the curious fantasies of a rule that will be no rule, mad Lear's "None does offend, none, I say none; I'll able 'em"; in Gonzalo's island dream in *The Tempest;* in Prospero's disqualification of himself as one able to bring order into other people's lives except through rituals of nature, affirmations of the rights of "wheat, rye, barley, vetches, oats, and peas."

But who of us will repine? "He who understands the masculine and keeps to the feminine shall become the whole world's channel. Eternal virtue shall not depart from him, and he shall return to the state of the infant."[27]

Notes to Chapter 2

1: ***P. 75.*** C. F. Tucker Brooke, whose historical scholarship has never been faulted, is worth quoting here: "So in Shakespeare's actual life he ignored the dreams of El Dorado and imperial England, and he ignored the facts of tobacco and the colonization of Virginia and the Fight of the Revenge, while scrutinizing day by day the thinking minds of the men and women about him. And thereby he gained a wisdom so deep that it concealed his plentiful lack of knowledge—a humanity so immense that few could note how completely he failed to be Elizabethan" ("Shakespeare Apart," *Essays on Shakespeare and Other Elizabethans,* New Haven, Yale University Press, 1948, p. 31).

2: ***P. 77.*** John Danby, *Shakespeare's Doctrine of Nature; A Study of King Lear* (London, 1949), p. 18. Compare with the earliest of all efforts at psychological study of the playwright: "We see these Characters act from the mingled motives of passion, reason, interest, habit and complection, in all their proportions, when they are supposed to know it not themselves," *An Essay on the Dramatic Character of Sir John Falstaff* (London, 1777), p. 67.

3: ***P. 78.*** In turning from impatience with Francis to thoughts of Hotspur—seeing himself as "not yet" enough of the latter's hue to differ much from Francis—Hal is life itself. Yet the likelihood of topical reference is also strong, for the remainder of the passage is obscure. Since the beginning of the 1590's the Earl of Essex had been enjoying as his chief source of income the imposts on all sweet wines drunk in England. Like Francis's, this sweet bondage had some five years to run, come Michaelmas (strictly, that would date the composition of the play before 1595), and one does not have to anticipate any of the future events, the queen's refusal to renew the license in 1600—the year of Essex's disgrace and ruin—to imagine this tax as a ready subject of conversation among those Londoners who, by drinking sack, some of them seasoning it with a pennyworth of sugared sonnet, helped keep the great earl in style. See the letter quoted by G. B. Harrison, *Life of Essex* (New York, 1937), pp. 132–133, in which Bacon condoled with Essex after the Cadiz expedition over Elizabeth's "inventions to keep your estate bare and low . . . thrusting you into odious employments and offices to supplant your reputation. . . ." Compare Essex's own complaints on this score made to Robert Cecil before the fleet set sail (*ibid.*, p. 102).

Let us now look at the concluding remarks to Francis: "Why then, your brown bastard is your only drink; for look you, Francis, your white canvas doublet will sully [the particular doublet was also worn by sailors]. In Barbary, sir, it cannot come to so much." Essex should know whether he was paying too high a price for his servitude; on the Cadiz expedition he had been party to the liberation of some wretched Turkish galley slaves and to the arranging of their passage to friendly Barbary ports. In Richard

Hakluyt's account, the event is followed by a fulsome tribute to Elizabeth as reputed deliverer of oppressed peoples throughout Christendom, concluding, "and therefore, whatsoever wicked designement shalbe conspired and plotted against her Majesty hereafter, shalbe thought to be conspired, plotted, and intended against the almighty himselfe: and for that cause, as I trust, shalbe by the infinite goodnes and mercy of that almighty, mightily frustrate and overthrowen" (*Principall Navigations,* New York, 1904, IV, 262).

4: ***P. 80.*** The clearest indication that Shakespeare was intent on more than dramatization of chronicles is seen in his assigning to Henry that personal coldness so well hit off by Falstaff in his praise of sack speech. In Holinshed we have a Henry who at first was unpopular by reason of "such taxes, tallages, subsidies, and exactions as he constreined to charge the people with" but "in his latter daies he shewed himselfe so gentle, that he gat more love amongst the nobles and people of this realme, than he had purchased malice and evill will in the beginning" (*Henry IV,* pp. 103–104). Shakespeare's Aumerle episode is developed from a bare sketch he may have read in Halle of the discovery of the plot, in which the duchess mother plays no part. See *A New Variorum Edition of Shakespeare, The Life and Death of King Richard II,* ed. Matthew W. Black (Philadelphia, 1955), pp. 451–452.

5: *P. 82.* Dover Wilson's remark (*The Fortunes of Falstaff* (Cambridge, 1943), p. 64, that his "attitude was perfect" throughout the interview, taken in conjunction with the assurance that the King at the time was "sick in body and spirit" (p. 61), suggests that a chivalrous son was sparing a sick father; this can only mean that Hal was in control of the interview, a view I am at pains to contest. There is no evidence of a sickly King Henry in Part I. The play begins with his provoking and facing down two powerful nobles and ends with his appearance in full armor in a battle where, as Holinshed said, "it is written" that he slew thirty-six rebels. Wilson was very likely remembering that other Holinshed statement that, at the time of the interview with his son, Henry was "greevouslie diseased." If so, he is in effect supposing that a London audience would be guided by what a few of them had read in Holinshed rather than what all were seeing enacted in the play. (Those same few might then be expected to remember that Holinshed had placed the interview *after* the battle of Shrewsbury in his account, not before.)

6: *P. 83.* *Both* differ from Holinshed in having the father dominate the interview. In Holinshed, the Prince came to court with a great train of supporters to set matters right concerning his reputed ill behavior. Though he did offer melodramatically to stab himself, yet, according to Holinshed, "by his great wisedome was the wrongfull suspicion which his father had conceived against him remooved, and he restored to his favour" (*Henry IV*, p. 97).

7: *P. 85.* There was precedent enough in Holinshed for a public meeting. The Prince had his retinue with him but commanded them not to approach "further than the fire in the same hall" (*Henry IV*, p. 95). In *Famous Victories*, after an argument, they were required to wait outside. In having Hal, as far as we can tell, completely unattended, Shakespeare was setting the stage for an event different from that of both his models.

8: *P. 86.* See Wilson's likening of the role-playing to the comic cradle scene in *The Second Shepherd's Play* (*Fortunes*, p. 136). The comparison is strained. Knowing that Hal "will turn out all right" hardly bears comparison with the seasonal solemnities of "Christ will be born, and all's well with the world." Cesar L. Barber, *Shakespeare's Festive Comedy* (Princeton, 1959), would have Falstaff's "Misrule" one of the devices for "charming away" certain "potential aberrations" confronting an heir apparent, his father's merely "magical majesty" (p. 178) and Hotspur's "intransigent chivalry" (p. 185). This, of course, would put Shakespeare on the side of that authority that traditionally granted choir boys an interval of misrule to the end of strengthening its own hold over them. I prefer, and I should think that the Church in its wisdom would also have preferred, a rationale that took into consideration the needs of the boys, their real need to ridicule authority. See J. Bronowski, *The Face of Violence* (London, 1954), pp. 18–19. Hal's confessing of his own aberrations publicly in a message to be carried to Hotspur on the eve of Shrewsbury reminds us that Hotspur was once a model held up to him by his father, a model now in as little esteem as he himself once had been.

9: ***P. 87.*** Taken from the speech of the King to the Prince's younger brother on his deathbed:

> His temper therefore must be well observ'd:
> Chide him for faults, and do it reverently,
> When you perceive his blood inclin'd to mirth . . .
> (2 *Henry IV* IV, iv, 36–38)

10: ***P. 87.*** The whole point of the Carrier Scene at Gadshill is to show that the Prince's activities smack of something more than high spirits and frivolity. The very look of one of his associates in the half-light of an inn court arouses suspicion in the breasts of honest folk.

11: ***P. 88.*** The public confession of his follies reported by Vernon on the eve of Shrewsbury is of an entirely different order. A youth's admission that he was *once* young can be made with characteristic missionary zeal:

And chid his truant youth with such a grace
As if he master'd there a double spirit
Of *teaching* and of learning instantly.
(V, ii, 62–64; *italics added*)

12: ***P. 89.*** *Quarto 1598 / A Facsimile in Foto-Lithography* (London, 1887), p. 21. There is more weeping before the famous crown-borrowing: ". . . but what shall I do? If weeping teares which come too late, may suffice the negligence neglected to some, I wil weepe day and night until the fountain be dry with weeping" (p. 23).

13: ***P. 90.*** It is pointed out by textual critics that the quarto printing of the lines includes the King's rejoinder on the same line of text:

. . . gracious lord,
Be more myself. KING: For all the world
As thou art now this hour was Richard then . . .

It is an unusual typographical liberty and may reflect a need to save paper. See Wilson's discussion, *Henry IV, Part I* (1946), pp. 103–107. I may point out, however, that the effect is to add impatience to an already impatient answer.

14: ***P. 94.*** Harold Jenkins, *The Structural Problem in Shake-*

speare's Henry The Fourth (London, 1956), p. 25. The lecture is addressed to the much-debated question of the continuity or lack of continuity between the two parts of *Henry IV*.

15: ***P. 97.*** "As so often in Shakespeare, the metaphors undo the logic and tell the truth over its head" (Harold C. Goddard, *The Meaning of Shakespeare,* Chicago, University of Chicago Press, 1951, p. 349). As a particular example of such "truth": "It has been argued that if repugnance to the act of killing had been the ground of Hamlet's hesitation he would have been conscious of the reason for his delay. But this is to forget the atmospheric pressure to which his mind was subjected. New moralities do not spring into existence in the face of intrenched custom in full-fledged conscious and conceptual force. They begin in dumb feelings around the heart ('thou wouldst not think how ill all's here about my heart') and in momentary gleams of the imagination" (*ibid.*, p. 345).

16: ***P. 97.*** "I know my friends are shaking their heads over me. They see me playing the fool and think me not capable of playing anything else. But they will one day find out their mistake. I don't mean all my days to be holidays spent among fools, however pleasant the holidays and however amusing the fools. And when I put on my working clothes and show the wiseacres what I really am and can do, they will give me all the more credit for it." The passage was quoted from John Bailey (*Shakespeare,* London, 1929) by Wilson, *Fortunes,* pp. 42–43, and given pride of place in G. Blakemore Evans, ed., *Supplement to Henry IV, Part I, A New Variorum Edition of Shakespeare* (*Shakespeare Quarterly*, VII [1956], 8).

17: ***P. 101.*** The lines:

> . . . I saw him dead,
> Breathless and bleeding on the ground.
> Art thou alive? or is it fantasy
> That plays upon our eyesight? I prithee, speak;
> We will not trust our eyes without our ears:
> Thou art not what thou seems't.
>
> (V, iv, 135–140)

are "comic" lines intended to go with some fairly broad stage business. The soliloquy earlier spoken over the sham corpse in rhyming couplets Wilson cites as the "tenderest expression" of friendship in the play (*Henry IV, Part I,* p. xii), rightly linking them with the lines spoken over the dead Hotspur. But a soliloquy in rhymed couplets is an extremely rare thing in Shakespeare and a sure sign, not of special sincerity, but of artifice, here the artifice of comedy. Hal knows that Falstaff is shamming, and thereto he "feeds" him appropriate lines about "embowelling." (Do we really take this reference to be accidental?) The terms on which these two understand each other are in deliberate contrast with the terms on which they do not understand King Henry and Prince John.

18: *P. 102. Henry IV*, p. 47.

19: *P. 103.* They are the *only* quarto lines omitted from the Folio. Dr. Johnson "suspected" that Shakespeare himself rejected them for reasons of inferior prosody.

20: *P. 108.* Merely compare with Holinshed's account: "The prince with a good audacitie, answered; 'Sir, to mine and all mens judgements you seemed dead in this world, wherefore I as your next heire apparant, tooke that as mine owne, and not as yours' " (*Henry IV*, p. 102). If one compares this with the *Famous Victories* version earlier cited, with its "weeping teares which come too late," (see Note 12), he will hardly fail to note that Shakespeare's is rather closer to *Famous Victories.* The sentiment was there, only asking to be shorn of its sentimentality.

21: *P. 109.* As many have noted, however, the King's very next words revert to policy: "God put it in thy mind to take it hence,/ That thou mightst win the more thy father's love,/Pleading so wisely in excuse of it." Here in epitome is a description of the King's own performance in the Audience Scene. It was a God-sent notion of his to have called his son a traitor and a coward.

22: *P. 110.* The failure of the Prince even to quote himself correctly when he reviews the death scene (IV, v, 157–163) has been taken as proof of his last-ditch hypocrisy. May I point out that he is quoting lines (*ibid.*, 22–30) which were actually spoken *before* he knew his father was dead, before he had applied the feather to his breath? Naturally, in retrospect he rephrases his thoughts to suit the difference, "remembering" that he had called the crown ("O polished perturbation! golden care!") a devourer of kings rather than a mere discomforter ("like a rich armour worn in heat of day", an appropriate thought *if* he supposed his father merely exhausted from his cares). I must frankly confess that I can find no difference in sincerity in the ring of the respective lines. Maybe Shakespeare made the mistake of having Hal speak "what we feel, not what we ought to say" (he ought of course to have been more consistent). The mind that as naturally as life catches such inconsistencies and records them defies understanding by most of us, who do well enough if we are consistent in our fixed ideas. Critics should, however, try a bit harder than the common run.

23: ***P. 115.*** That so many of the learned world have taken Falstaff to their hearts as the very Absolute of Irresponsibility is not for me, a member myself, to comment on. Women, I suspect, have an instinctive dislike of him, with good reason if we think of his treatment of Dame Quickly. Furthermore, he is held to be proud by the tavern servitors, a very damning charge in these plays. Consider the fine and instinctive courtesy shown Dame Quickly by Prince Hal. Entranced as one may be by Falstaff, it is hard to overlook the facts: Shakespeare confers on him as many of the traits of the tyrant as he confers of the natural democrat on Hal.

24: ***P. 117.*** The blaming of others for failing to equal oneself in magnanimity makes for two, to my mind, very wasteful plays, wasteful of psychic energy. I refer to *Coriolanus* and *Timon.* The impulse throughout the whole of *Timon* and throughout one scene of *Henry V* (the extraordinary tirade of II, ii, 79–144) to make others pay for ingratitude that reads suspiciously as if it had been invited by the injured party himself bespeaks a trait in Shakespeare that would bear investigation by the properly qualified. To justify such plays and scenes to the last particle on dramatic grounds I find impossible (and it is the last particle that has to be taken into account).

25: ***P. 118.*** *Face of Violence,* p. 15.

26: ***P. 118.*** The "mystery" ("with whom relation/Durst never meddle—in the soul of state," *Troilus and Cressida,* III, iii, 202–203) stands revealed as nothing more than superior espionage work, and not a very exalted kind at that. It is known to the Greek high command that Achilles has a sweetheart in Troy. There is kinship with the usage in *Othello,* in the scene in which Othello pretends to Emilia that she is the proprietess of a brothel ("Cough or cry 'hem' if any body come;/ Your mystery, your mystery; nay, dispatch," IV, ii, 28–29). As for Lear's proposal to Cordelia that they act as "God's spies," observing "Who loses and who wins;

who's in, who's out;/And take upon's the mystery of things" (V, iii, 15–16), in the context of that bitter play, the only response is, "Who cares?"

27: *P. 118.* This quotation from the *Upanishads* I owe to Professor Goddard, in his chapter on *Hamlet* in *The Meaning of Shakespeare,* p. 333.

3 *Some Undercover Literary Skirmishing*

What has been revealed in the two previous chapters will now appear as representing more a habit of mind than any conscious program if we turn to two examples of the same sort of activity where the consequences of "subversion" were either slight or almost nonexistent. Both are taken from the comedies. The first amounts to a fairly good-humored reflection on the behavior of the influential Tudor patron of art, with whom, from any evidence we have, Shakespeare could not have had any great quarrel. The play is *A Midsummer-Night's Dream.* The second is far more concealed and biting reflection, yet good-humored, too, in its way, on certain theatre practices that were becoming fashionable at the end of his career as playwright. The play is *The Winter's Tale.*

To sum up: at the beginning of his career, we see Shakespeare responding to a threat to his craft from the outside, as it were, the threat of fundamental disbelief in the craft itself (we may call it Philistinism in high places). At the end of his career, we see him responding to a threat from within, to an encroaching decadence abetted by its very practitioners.

A Midsummer-Night's Dream is a play entirely monopolized by "revels." There are the official revels ordered by Theseus, Duke of Athens, to celebrate his coming nuptials with Hippolyta, Queen of the Amazons; and there are the spontaneous revels that erupt on the bidding of no one else on earth. The humor of the play turns on the contrasting behavior of the fashionable Athenians toward other people's foolishness, as displayed in the official revels, and the tolerant forgetfulness they show toward their own, in the unofficial. As involuntary participants in an art experience, they are under the direct control of Dionysus, or—if you prefer the Elizabethan term—of fairyland.

Let us examine at some length the credentials of the group who, before the play is through, will pass judgment on the taste and competence of certain tradesmen, their social inferiors. We need go no further than their leader the Duke of Athens, since it is from him that they take their cue. As we all know, this Duke has long been credited with framing one of the classic definitions of *poesis*, "making," the famous poet's-pen speech. Before we turn to it, I think it should be remarked how little at home this honorable, and on the whole sympathetic, figure is in the world of Dionysus. How urbanely Shakespeare makes the point when he puts into his mouth, and the mouth of his bride-to-be, that superb duet of appreciation of the music of hounds, music heard in the early morning when the manly sun has begun to chase away the mists, uncertainties, and terrors of moonlight. Shakespeare, we cannot help feeling, must have had a tenderness for a certain kind of extrovert to write such lines for them, Hotspurs and Mercutios, men of lively but no very individual feeling. Mercutio's Queen Mab speech is better admired for its nonchalant virtuosity than for any delicate appositeness to life. Much as we enjoy it, we note that it conveys very little about dreams. They are "nothing," perhaps a matter of what one ate before going to sleep, to put it at its crudest. The dreams he cites are literal waking thoughts, not the sort that plagued Macbeth and his wife, we may be sure. One has a shrewd suspicion that the Queen Mab speech was originally written for someone in *A Midsummer-Night's Dream,* perhaps Duke Theseus—it has little point in the play *Romeo and Juliet.*

Shakespeare wanted a graver speech for Theseus and yet one in which it would be clear to some, at least, that the good man did not entirely know what he was talking about. Like many another, he was repeating things that he had heard, to which he had probably given very little thought. Here is the famous poet's-pen speech in its entirety; Theseus is accounting for the experience of the four lovers in the woods outside Athens:

> More strange than true. I never may believe
> These antique fables, nor these fairy toys.
> Lovers and madmen have such seething brains,
> Such shaping fantasies, that apprehend
> More than cool reason ever comprehends.
> The lunatic, the lover, and the poet,
> Are of imagination all compact:

One sees more devils than vast hell can hold,
That is, the madman; the lover, all as frantic,
Sees Helen's beauty in a brow of Egypt:
The poet's eye, in a fine frenzy rolling,
Doth glance from heaven to earth, from earth to heaven;
And, as imagination bodies forth
The forms of things unknown, the poet's pen
Turns them to shapes, and gives to airy nothing
A local habitation and a name.
Such tricks hath strong imagination,
That, if it would but apprehend some joy,
It comprehends some bringer of that joy;
Or in the night, imagining some fear,
How easy is a bush suppos'd a bear!

(V, i, 2–22)

As with Jacques's Seven Ages of Man speech, the felicitous gravity of this discourse long ago caught the world's fancy—clear shallows have been gazed into as if they were authentic Shakespearean depths. (For a few, the solution to the lameness of the final couplets is to add them to the list of lines that Shakespeare "couldn't have written.") In all seriousness, what are these depths? They seem to amount to this: there is a certain class of people who see what "isn't there," who make something out of nothing.[1] It is a fairly commonplace notion and certainly not true of poets, however it may be of lovers and madmen. Yet it is hard to contest your graver sort of Philistine—a *fine* frenzy, mind you, but still a frenzy and therefore not to be encouraged *too far*. Or—"forget it, it's all in your imagination." As Theseus would say, "Just wait until morning." (To quote Plato's *Ion* in support of Theseus—as has been done—is little to the point, Plato being in matters of art quite content to be the prince of Philistines.)

Wait until morning: precisely, of course, what the poet would not have us do! It is *there*, in moonlight, that we remake the world in accordance with our secret wishes, be they wishes of terror or wishes of delight. Moonlight is where primordial making occurs. Did not Wordsworth and Coleridge long ago urge upon us that moonlight perception is that perception in which we must will *not* to disbelieve if we are to be fully alive? On a deeper level than bushes and bears—though Peter Bell is not the very best example—our lives are changed by imaginative experience. We are to some degree the poorer if they are not. In Shakespeare's play, Bottom, an ordinary sensitive man, has an experience that must forever remain private to him. It is a pity, for it is certain that he *was* in fairyland for a time:

> . . . The eye of man hath not heard, the ear of man hath not seen, man's hand is not able to taste, his tongue to conceive,

nor his heart to report, what my dream was. I will get Peter Quince to write a ballad of this dream: it shall be called Bottom's Dream, because it hath no bottom; and I will sing it in the latter end of a play, before the Duke: peradventure, to make it the more gracious, I shall sing it at her death.

(IV, i, 218–226)

Such self-importance, of course, is comic and moves us to laughter. As I have already observed, however, there is comedy of a more equivocal sort yet to come, comedy not at the expense of comic "types" acting out of their sphere, but at the expense of their betters who presume to laugh at them. Not for nothing has Shakespeare in the early scenes juxtaposed their *un*-rehearsed tragi-comedy in all its mistaken seriousness with the rehearsal of the piece that they are later to see and laugh at.

Before proceeding further, however, it is well to meet a likely objection. How, one might ask, does this compounded sort of humor differ in any significant way from the quite harmless fun of the comedy preceding this one, *Love's Labour's Lost*? I can only reply that the intent of the two seems totally different, however similar the dramatic devices employed. In one particular, Shakespeare seems to have moved backward, when, in the play as a whole, he was moving forward. In *A Midsummer-Night's Dream*, a superior play in every way, the witty obbligato provided by the in-group, the so-to-speak intellectual elite, is almost oppressively sophomoric. Not by any means is this so in *Love's Labour's Lost,* where a dazzling spectrum of wit, ranging from silly puns to the most elegant of verbal fencing, matches a social pecking order in which ultimately no one (except the women) is spared—clown, pedant, or *haut monde.* At the end, it falls to the women—so vulnerable to poetry, so besieged by it, and usually so little concerned with its manufacture—to pass judgment upon the sublunaries, the supposed winners of the previous contests, who by now will want to forget the whole thing as a bad dream. How different all this in the next play, where fully half the characters are unaware to the very end of the parts they have been playing: "Lord, what fools these mortals be!"

Much of the charm of *Love's Labour's Lost* lies in the feeling it arouses in us that the actors are going about their business on stage as if for their own amusement—there is kinship here with the coming great comedies—we the paying audience being present only by accident, and lucky to be present! On the contrary, our presence at *A Midsummer-Night's Dream* is essential. Except for the fairies, we are the only ones in a position to say what has happened. Without us, there can hardly be said to have been a play. And if, by the same token, there are any judgments to be passed, it being the way of comedies to invite such judgments, we are the only ones in a position to pass them. Let us proceed to such a judgment now. Is there any one of us who would not trade all the witticisms and interruptions of Theseus and court for another five minutes of

> A tedious brief scene of young Pyramus
> And his love Thisbe; very tragical mirth?
> (V, i, 56–58)

Crude as it is, the play's the thing, and we would have more of it rather than less. I cannot imagine anyone's wanting more of the interruptions. (Incidentally, we might recall that Shakespeare must have known only too well what it was like to have one's faithfully conned lines, delivered the best one knew how, continually interrupted by some silly ass on an opera chair who would presently wander off to place a bet in a howling bear pit, or perhaps merely yawn and scratch himself.)

One's appetite for the Pyramuses and Thisbes of the stage, for amateur productions in general, varies directly, let us say, with their mythopoeic content, with the amount of *literal* naïve belief the actors appear to have in what they are doing. Surely, few actors ever made a greater investment of such belief than the group of tradesmen who gathered in the woods outside Athens to rehearse the play they hoped to give before their duke and his court. It was a great blunder to give "Wall" lines to speak. Children might make such a blunder. On the other hand, to warn an audience in advance that a lion is not a real lion, but an actor, is not so much a case of ignorance of dramatic canons, as the graver critics would have it, as the working of *mimesis,* in its stoutest if not its purest form. We will forgive much for this. (Nor should we forget that Shakespeare was exaggerating.)

On the festive night, to an accompaniment little better than muted catcalls, the playlet was presented. Halfway through, Hippolyta, for one, found she had had enough:

> HIPPOLYTA. This is the silliest stuff that ever I heard.
>
> THESEUS. The best in this kind are but shadows, and the worst are no worse, if imagination amend them.
>
> HIPPOLYTA. It must be your imagination then, and not theirs.
>
> (*Ibid.,* 214–218)

Verily, we are such stuff as dreams are made on, and our little life is rounded with a sleep! Prospero might be forgiven such valedictory sentiments, but hardly Theseus, this early morning hunter, this dismisser of night happenings. What does he know of the shadows that come with the death of each day's life, not to mention those thrown up by eternity? Yet how often and admiringly have the above lines of Theseus been quoted, and in what humanitarian contexts, too! No doubt of it: he liked the sound of the words as much as we do. But happier for Bottom, Quince, and the rest had he shown some small disposition to put them into practice. Or am I being sentimental? Must we suppose the group of such dull wit as not to know the difference, not to have been grateful for tokens of the ducal imagination at work amending their efforts instead of ridiculing them? [2]

Theseus's last words are that "Pyramus and Thisbe" would make a fine tragedy if the author of it were to hang himself in the leading lady's garter. He notes that the hour is late. "This palpable-gross play hath well beguil'd/The heavy gait of night." It is time for bed.

It was no part of Shakespeare's purpose to supply ammunition for future Marxist thought, but it is, nevertheless, worth remembering that a brother writer of great stature, writing at this time of a ducal court in Spain, depicted a scene not far from Shakespeare's in its social commentary. I refer to the episode in Cervantes' *Don Quixote* that seems to have been deliberately designed to provoke reflection over the seeming fact that a number of high-born persons have no better use for their time than to use it in devising an elaborate hoax, that of shaving off the beard of an errant knight. An amusing enough figure, the gentle Don, but at the same time their undoubted moral superior. It was his poverty and somewhat lower social position that qualified him for the treatment, just as it was social position and ignorance that qualified Bottom and his fellow tradesmen. In Shakespeare's scenes, of course, there is far less implicit bitterness, perhaps no bitterness at all. Nevertheless, they do raise an uneasy thought or two about the certainty of finding either developed taste or developed feeling in company with high social position. It is an uneasiness not unwarranted when the times were those of a newly created Tudor aristocracy.

Before moving on to the next play, I must enter a reminder. In the foregoing, the play *A Midsummer-Night's Dream* has by no means been "explained." At most, something has been explained about its author. The play, like all good plays, has a life of its own apart from the author's interests and ends. I ask that this be kept in mind equally for *The Winter's Tale*.

2

One can say many things about melodrama. It is a bastard product of art, but if it is properly behaved it can often be as interesting as its legitimate kin. If it has any discoverable antecedents, they are to be sought in primitive initiation ceremonies designed to give the immature an assurance that they are ready to cope with adult responsibilities of hunting, killing, and procreation. Conducted by the elders of the group, they provide the young with fictitious trials that they will later encounter in earnest. In societies that have already had the experience of tragedy, the reversion to melodrama, or tragi-comedy, represents a willed return to adolescence. Melodrama tells us that life's hardships are overcome by happy coincidence, by improbable changes in someone's heart, or merely by wishing them away. Comedy does these things too, but with the understanding that the hardships are not real ones to begin with—they are fairy-tale or bookish. Melodrama makes exaggerated efforts to convince us of the opposite, both by ultrarealism of event, bereavements, widowings, injustices, savage tyrannies—all circumstantial, all as life has taught us to know them—and, when it is permitted, by acute psychological analysis. The all-important "truth," as it dawns on us in melodrama, not too rapidly in the best melodramas, is that we *need* not have been upset, that it was not as we thought, that all will turn out well in the end. We signal our relief to each other by social tears of relief and, simultaneously, our hatred of those who have manipulated us, by social laughter.

At the end of Shakespeare's dramatic career, melodrama was taking the place of tragedy as serious entertainment. The move of the theatres indoors may have had something to do with it, for the greater comfort indoors encourages passivity, letting things happen to one rather than participating in them. John Fletcher was the popular tragi-comic playwright then writing for the

Blackfriars Theatre, in which Shakespeare had a financial interest. For whatever reason we can suppose, he began collaborating with Fletcher on plays for Blackfriars. It was probably not his financial need so much as that of the new company. He had outlived, professionally, many of his compeers, and it is easy to imagine that he liked the youth, vitality, and experimentation of the newer set. About 1610, he produced the play *Cymbeline,* which in inimitable Shakespearean fashion outdid all other melodramas. But he never went so far again: a girl embracing a headless corpse under the impression that it is the body of her lover when in reality it is that of her would-be ravisher; the same girl in the disguise of a page struck to the ground by her real lover for having interrupted him in a conversation. There is evidence that *Cymbeline* was played at Blackfriars.

Shakespeare's next effort at tragi-comedy or melodrama was *The Winter's Tale,* a play that represents a vast retreat from *Cymbeline* in the direction of serious, rather than haphazard, dramaturgy. If the word means anything, it is in every sense a more serious play, this despite the fact that it contains as much of the new mode as of the old. If it was played at the Globe instead of Blackfriars,[3] comedy might be said to be back on home ground. Some, at least, of the spectators would have fond recollections of an earlier pastoral comedy, the innocent *As You Like It.*

Entitled *"The" Winter's Tale,* not *"A" Winter's Tale,* it will be seen to represent an effort to prove that the good old comedy was not *perdita,* "lost," but very much alive and very able to take care of herself. At its conclusion, Shakespeare resurrects in all serenity a wrinkled (it is true) but still very beautiful Thalia, Muse of Comedy:

> When she was young you woo'd her; now in age
> Is she become the suitor!
>
> (V, iii, 108–109)

The playful but half severe charge is spoken to Leontes, whose unreasoning jealousy at the start of the play had brought this near divinity to the edge of death. But that is long past. Her child, the babe Perdita, has in the meantime grown to maturity—in healthier surroundings than her father's effete court. She has but recently been discovered and her parentage made known to the world. As an incredulous waiting-gentleman says:

> Women will love her, that she is a woman
> More worth than any man; men, that she is
> The rarest of all women.
>
> (V, i, 111–113)

If this is so, something is to be seen on the stage that has become a bit uncommon. In Stuart drama, the lines between the sexes, as well as between professions, blood-relationships, and fealties, have become badly blurred.[4]

None of this, I believe, will be very doggedly contested by those who know the play. It is a possible interpretation. What has not been previously noted is that Shakespeare, in addition to resurrecting the old comedy for one wonderful hour, has also interjected a between-the-lines indictment of his associates who were responsible for her being lost—and it goes without saying, of the public whose questionable taste has supplied the encouragement. Perhaps he was answering the tolerant charge, "You are old, Father William," and is showing to anyone interested that *his* Winter's Tale is still worth the telling. If some of the elements of this Winter's Tale will be a travesty of good art, perhaps future generations will be able to tell the difference. At any rate, there is much in Shakespeare's *The Winter's Tale* that has never been fully explained to anyone's satisfaction, and I propose to make the effort to explain it.

First and last is the puzzling lecture of Perdita to two older men on the nature of gillyflowers, following the attempt of one of them to persuade her that such transplants represent a "higher" art of gardening. What does Shakespeare mean by letting his plot idle while this unimportant question is argued, and argued at length—and is brought to no conclusion? I imagine that the followers of Fletcher were very good at similar theoretical arguments to justify the popular art form they were evolving. Admitted that some of the effects were extreme, do they not deserve, nevertheless, to be called art, no less than the forced yield of an orchard that has benefited from grafting operations deserves to be called Nature's handiwork, perhaps even a higher handiwork? They could read from George or Richard Puttenham's treatise *The Arte of English Poesie,* citing gillyflowers as an example of what the gardener-poet can do to further nature's "conclusions," thereby to "make her effects more absolute and straunge." [5] To what if *not* to art is owing the new luxuriance of the stage? Let taste but keep pace and the theatres are assured a rich growth of harmless entertainment. (There is not space to devote to summaries of Fletcher plots; suffice it to say that the reader who has an appetite for unlikely happenings, strained relations, and, above all, what we should call abnormal psychology will find it satisfied, as far as old plays can satisfy it, by the plots and characterizations of Fletcher.)

Shakespeare was not entirely a newcomer to the field. In *The Winter's Tale* itself, some elements, if allowed to dominate the whole, would have made for something more extreme even than *Cymbeline,* which for all its involutions is basically very simple in intent. I have in mind the overripe relationship between

Leontes and Polixenes, a far cry from the marmoreal nobility of the masculine friendship in *Julius Caesar,* for example. It is suspiciously like the Amintor-Melantius friendship of the current Fletcher success *The Maid's Tragedy.* (If there is imitation, there is little doubt who was imitating whom.) Even more suspect is the much commented-on jealousy of Leontes, as different in its suddenness and violence from the affliction of a Lear as pathological manifestations are from mythological—in folklore, as Aristotle intimated, improbabilities receive sanction from the very weight of the "it is said." There is nothing like the jealousy of Leontes in the rest of Shakespeare.

Given the extraordinary Protean character of the author—the world has not seen its like—we are justified in pursuing a line of inquiry that may seem overworked to a generation brought up on earnest symbol-searching in literary interpretation. I trust that the difference will be detected.

Jealousy, the general class of feeling of which sexual jealousy is but a species, arises from a dread that the one nearest and dearest to one cannot be trusted. Conceivably, then, it might be associated with a middle-aged poet accustomed to observing the conduct of his muse in the company of other men, those contemporaries and predecessors whose writing, the textbooks tell us, has "influenced" him. It may be a minor emotion, but we call it so at our own risk. The very conception of a muse as something that visits, surprises, and occasionally betrays an author prohibits the thought that she is ever owned. And yet a man feels that she is peculiarly his own. Early in *The Winter's Tale* an offspring is born. Whose is it?

> And thou, good goddess Nature, which hast made it
> So like to him that got it, if thou hast
> The ordering of the mind too, 'mongst all colours
> No yellow in't; lest she suspect, as he does,
> Her children not her husband's.
>
> (II, iii, 103–107)

This is the prayer of the waiting gentlewoman, who shortly takes it upon herself to save both mother and child from the jealous fury of the father, an odd prayer indeed if it is a human child actually in question. It is not impossible that a woman will at some time or other be concerned about the legitimacy of her offspring, but we should want to know the circumstances before we took the idea very seriously. On the other hand, for an art form to be so "concerned" is not strange in the least. Unless we object on fundamental grounds to the metaphor itself, we must grant that art is very much concerned about the consequences to itself of various experiments, adulterations, hybridizations, and such. This babe may be quite vitally concerned one day with who "breeds" by her (her own word sixteen years hence).

The play will leap the sixteen years at the end of Act III, and Perdita will be put to the test in a debate, a debate about horticulture, of all things. The critics who have labeled this part of the play The Great Debate may not be so far wrong as they thought. We shall return to the point in a moment.

The crowning achievement of melodrama is without doubt the chain of thrills and surprises brought to conclusion in the last act. Now for all the potential surprises of *The Winter's Tale* to be packed properly into Act V (as in *Cymbeline*) required everyone's presence back in Sicily, where the play's action commenced. This in turn required an elopement out of Bohemia by Perdita and and her lover Florizel and a pursuit by an enraged king, Florizel's father. Readers of the play do not have to be told that nothing further is heard of Polixenes' mighty choler once it has served its turn in Act IV. It is not for melodrama to make unnecessary difficulties out of motivation. One simply accepts the fact that a son has suddenly said something "unfilial," and a father becomes as suddenly "tyrannical," after which they return to normal. Fletcher's plays are held together by such character motivation. Before the present act, there had been no reason to think of

Polixenes as anything but "a holy father/A graceful gentleman" (V, i, 170–171), whose mistreatment by his best friend had forced him into a role of passive suffering and confined him to speeches of sorrow and anxiety. Only a moment before, he had been observing the two young people, disguised as a benevolent onlooker of their rustic sheep-shearing. Now he becomes one to disown a son and threaten a hapless girl with disfigurement ("I'll have thy beauty scratch'd with briers . . . I will devise a death as cruel for thee/As thou art tender to't"). Indeed, we are a long way from the genial stoicism of the banished Duke in *As You Like It.*

Let us pass over the steps by which Florizel and Perdita are got out of Bohemia. They are not easy to recall unless it be that one has read the play the night before. Let us rather turn to the debate with Polixenes over flowers before the quarrel with the undutiful son breaks out. All present are in one form or another of disguise. Perdita is distributing appropriate flowers to the guests of her adopted shepherd-father's guests. Like Chlorin in Fletcher's *Faithful Shepherdess,* Perdita, versed in both herblore and chastity, is qualified to give the law to all comers. Polixenes humorously remonstrates with her about the ascription to him and his aged companion Camillo of flowers of winter—rosemary and rue—which "keep/Seeming and savour all the winter long." The following dialogue ensues:

PERDITA. Sir, the year growing ancient,
Not yet on summer's death, nor on the birth
Of trembling winter, the fairest flowers o' the season
Are our carnations, and streak'd gillyvors,
Which some call nature's bastards: of that kind
Our rustic garden's barren, and I care not
To get slips of them.

POLIXENES. Wherefore, gentle maiden,
Do you neglect them?

PERDITA. For I have heard it said
There is an art which in their piedness shares
With great creating nature.

POLIXENES. Say there be;
Yet nature is made better by no mean
But nature makes that mean: so, over that art,
Which you say adds to nature, is an art
That nature makes. You see, sweet maid, we marry
A gentler scion to the wildest stock,
And make conceive a bark of baser kind
By bud of nobler race: this is an art
Which does mend nature, change it rather, but
The art itself is nature.

PERDITA. So it is.

POLIXENES. Then make your garden rich in gillyvors,

And do not call them bastards.

PERDITA. I'll not put
The dibble in earth to set one slip of them;
No more than, were I painted, I would wish
This youth should say, 'twere well, and only therefore
Desire to breed by me. Here's flowers for you;
Hot lavender, mints, savory, marjoram;
The marigold, that goes to bed wi' the sun,
And with him rises weeping: these are flowers
Of middle summer, and I think they are given
To men of middle age. You're very welcome.

(IV, iii, 79–108)

For the playwright who fathered her, and for great creating Nature, too, the courageous independence shown by his offspring is of far greater moment than anything she is likely to find required of her as the "Perdita" of the plot. In one way or another, she will be seen to be a king's daughter, for that is the nature of pastoral tales. As a matter of fact, there are only fifty or so lines left for her to speak in the entire play. Greater things are at stake in this comedy than a lost princess. In the *un*winter and *un*summer of the new Blackfriars theatre, what of *the breed* itself? Will it be able to maintain its pure lineage in the face of, among other things, outlandish plot requirements? Little may Perdita know it, but one is speaking through her mouth with an urgency she cannot suspect, Thalia, Muse of Comedy.

> . . . when you do dance, I wish you
> A wave o' the sea, that you might ever do
> Nothing but that; move still, still so,
> And own no other function . . .
> (IV, iii, 140–144)

The extraordinary idealism of these lines suggests no ordinary lover, and Florizel, who speaks them, is no different from other Shakespearean lovers of comedy. May it not be the author, in love, as he so often seems in his sonnets, with his own creation?

The ambiguous passage back in Act II has anticipated the theme of bastardy, but only anticipated it. Here it is made to reveal its full particularity.[6] The child of Act III, now grown to womanhood, must play a part in the all-important fifth act of a tragi-comedy. Already chosen by a highborn youth for qualities that are the opposite of fashionable, she has made it clear to the youth's father that she is stubbornly jealous of her stock. There will be no illegitimate growths in *her* plot if she has anything to say about it. It must be remembered that in the original story, the prose romance *Pandosto* of Robert Greene, a king had mistakenly conceived an incestuous passion for his own daughter on her return to her place of birth, then, learning her identity, had committed suicide. This particular "gillyvor" [7] is something that neither she nor Shakespeare will ever consent to. Sensationalism in fifth acts was carried as far as it was going to be carried in the preceding play, *Cymbeline*.

And yet there are considerations of plain business sense. The day is obviously past when an audience can be expected to be amused of an afternoon, like the Globe audience, by the spectacle, say, of a Duke's *half*-sensing (we cannot be sure) that the youth he is talking to is his own daughter in disguise, his deliciously keeping up the pretense—for what? Simply for the sake of participating in comedy. It behooved the author, then, to create enough excitement in his fifth act to suit the sophisticated tastes of the times and yet sacrifice none of his principles.

He struck a compromise. The denouement of *The Winter's Tale* is neither raw *Pandosto* nor the innocent spoofing of *As You Like It*—what spoofing there is is significantly broad. It ends, as expected, in a whirl of excitement; but the excitement is magically transferred to a theme by now almost forgotten, the child's mother. Dare we call her a resurrected muse of Old Comedy, worn by years but still most beautiful and most compelling of homage? This surprise of Shakespeare's is like no other in all his plays, finding an audience completely unprepared, completely surprising them. At the same time, it is of so solemn a nature that it obliterates memory of all preceding surprises, that sequence of events that an audience at a melodrama has been warned to expect—revelations in rapid succession, cries of joy, swooning, tears, laughter. Undoubtedly, these scenes have come perilously close to parody, if they are not the thing itself, and Shakespeare has planted them liberally. But they are only nominal gillyflowers, and he seems not to care how they grow.[8] The play hastens to another conclusion.

The foregoing account of a kind of skirmishing in *The Winter's Tale* would hardly bear comparison with that of *A Midsummer-Night's Dream* if this were all. There is lacking yet some such *coup de grâce* as finished off the good Duke Theseus, whose utterly innocent and unconscious failure to live up to his high-minded professions in effect left nothing more to be said for him. Let us return to the gillyflower passage and run our thumbs over an edge that once upon a time drew fraternal blood, though over the years it has been somewhat overlaid with the rust of scholarly footnotes.

"We" [that is to say, if "we" are Polixenes-Fletcher, our collaborators] may indeed *talk* of improving on Nature by resort to grafting operations, but it turns out to be only idle talk, no practice. No, when it comes to practice, "we" are not found to be so wonderfully democratic. For let us suppose—and the evidence is far from clear (take our current *Maid's Tragedy*, for example)—

anyway, let us suppose, that we know the difference between queenly and servant-girl deportment: why are we so suddenly averse to letting Nature assume the risks in an instance like the present? If the art itself *is* Nature, the match with our well-born son will prove a happy one. On the other hand, if there is such an estrangement between court and country—and it was not so in my day—what on earth are you and I doing writing pastoral comedies? Please tell me that. And in this same connection, is it really necessary for this king Polixenes to become so furiously angry, so "absolute and strange" in his wrath? My dear fellow, where will it lead us, this headlong abandonment of principle at every little offer of surprise and extra thrill that occurs to us?

Annihilating humor this. (Though hardly to be compared in daring with calling one's sovereign a Welsh bully.) But it is a humor that is not basically unkind, not inconsistent with loyalty and friendship. *Labuntur anni.* If there is an undercurrent of sadness, there is also a humorous acceptance of realities: as Horace said, *Nos nequiores mox daturos/Progeniem vitiosiorem*—"the next generation is always going to the dogs." "So it is," says Perdita, in answer to the argument that some higher type of art is in the making. She will not argue the point. No more will Shakespeare. Let the younger ones have it their way. It is their world too, and one cannot live forever. Let grace and remembrance by all means be the marks of old age.

Before we are through, though, let us hear once again the names of those flowers of hot summer and of spring. Then, in a moment, we are listening to lines of almost intolerable beauty, the wave o' the sea passage already quoted, the winds of March passage preceding. It is beauty *poured on*, a lark at heaven's gate singing. If a young contemporary had happened to hint more or less inadvertently, "You are old, Father William," he might well now have reason to wish for a little of that eld himself. Fitting it is for *The Winter's Tale* to conclude the roster of comedies in the First Folio of Shakespeare's plays!

"Take your sweetheart's hat," says old Camillo, who abets the elopement of Perdita and Florizel:

> And pluck it o'er your brows; muffle your face;
> Dismantle you, and, as you can, disliken
> The truth of your own seeming; that you may,—
> For I do fear eyes over you,—to shipboard
> Get undescried.
>
> PERDITA. I see the play so lies
> That I must bear a part.
>
> CAMILLO. No remedy. . . .
>
> (IV, iii, 667–671)

. . . or, as the Chorus *Time* announces at the beginning of the Act that has occupied us so:

Let me pass
The same I am, ere ancient'st order was
Or what is now receiv'd: I witness to
The times that brought them in; so shall I do
To the freshest things now reigning, and make stale
The glistering of this present, as my tale
Now seems to it.

(IV, 9–13)

Notes to Chapter 3

1: ***P. 136.*** Sonnet 114 contains the Shakespearean equivalent of the famous Romantic doctrine of Imagination. In associating love with *flattery* of the mind rather than with *deception,* Shakespeare precludes the something-out-of-nothing (out of base matter, alchemically speaking) or all-in-the-eye explanation of love. The extension to poetry is obvious; the mind is a willing partner in a suspension of disbelief, even when it knows (and Shakespeare is insistent on the point) that the flattering eye may be conveying a message as disturbing as poison.

2: ***P. 141.*** Theseus has earlier confided to Hippolyta that he has often in the past suffered through the ceremonial visits of burgomasters, scholars, and the like and has taken pains to conceal his impatience with their tiresome addresses. Such folk were, of course, his lettered inferiors, whereas Bottom and company were unlettered.

3: ***P. 144.*** It was seen "at the glob" by a contemporary on May 15, 1611, Simon Foreman, physician and astrologer.

4: ***P. 146.*** The loss of all sense of decorum is the hallmark of the new Stuart drama. There is no country fellow in all of Shakespeare faintly resembling the country fellow in *Philaster,* who seeing a maiden threatened by a gallant with drawn sword, drives the latter away most chivalrously, it is true, but only to conceive the notion immediately thereafter of attacking her himself in his own fashion. Nor is there a gallant like Philaster, who goes off muttering after this defeat that he would not have been so easily intimidated if he had been feeling more himself.

5: *P. 147.* I am indebted for this contemporary reference to J. H. P. Pafford, ed., *The Winter's Tale* (1963), p. 170.

6: *P. 154.* Needless to say, it has exercised readers to think of an occasion when a woman would be "jealous" of her husband in this particular way, suspecting her children not his.

7: *P. 155.* A bit of rueful joking in V, i, 224–227 is all that remains of the *Pandosto* episode. The Fletcherian laugh that may have been invited is quickly enough checked by a reference to Hermione.

8: *P. 156.* He has dug up one from older comedy too and planted it earlier, at the end of Act III, the famous *Exit* [of Antigonus], *pursued by a bear.* (There are so many pursuing bears in *Mucedorus,* at least in the 1611 version that has come down to us, that one of the characters in that play asks where they all come from.) For all the efforts of critics to give significance to the episode, I cannot see that Shakespeare meant it as anything but parody, particularly the lines, "I'll go see if the bear be gone from the gentleman, and how much he hath eaten" (III, iii, 132–134). That Shakespeare may have had *Mucedorus* in mind while writing *The Winter's Tale* is supported by a line in the former, in which Mucedorus, deciding to disguise himself as a shepherd, professes to have a mind "grafted on an humbler stock".

APPENDIX

The following passages from Holinshed speak eloquently of the material Shakespeare had at hand to work into his play—if he had wanted to. The first four of them are from the articles of peace:

> 9 Also we to our power shall defend and helpe all and everie of the peeres, nobles, cities, townes, communalties, and singular persons, now or in time comming, subjects to our father [his French father-in-law-to-be] in their rights, customes, privileges, freedomes, and franchises, longing or due to them in all manner of places now or in time comming subject to our father.
>
> (*Henry V*, p. 99)

> 10 Also we diligentlie and truelie shall travell to our power, and doo that justice be administred and doone in the same realme of France after the lawes, customes, and rights of the same realme, without personall exception. And that we shall keepe and hold the subjects of the same realme in tranquillitie and peace, and to our power we shall defend them against all manner of violence and oppression.
>
> (*Ibid.*)

> 28 Also that thenceforward, perpetuallie, shall be still rest, and that in all maner of wise, dissentions, hates, rancors,

envies and wars, betweene the same realmes of France and England, and the people, of the same realmes, drawing to accord of the same peace, may cease and be broken.

(*Ibid.*, p. 103)

29 Also that there shall be from henceforward for evermore, peace, and tranquillitie, and good accord and common affection, and stable friendship betweene the said realmes, and their subjects before said. The same realmes shall keepe themselves with their councell, helps, and common assistance against all maner of men that inforce them for to dooen or to imagine wrongs, harmes, displeasures, or grievances to them or either of them. . . .

(*Ibid.*)

During the time that the two kings thus sojourned in Paris, the French king kept a small port, verie few, and those of the meaner sort resorting unto his court: but the king of England kept such a solemne state, with so plentifull an house, and shewed himselfe so bountifull in gifts, and setting foorth of warlike shewes and princelie pastimes, that all the noble men and other resorted to his palace, to see his estate, and to doo him honor.

(*Ibid.*, pp. 113–114)

. . . This Henrie was a king, of life without spot, a prince whome all men loved, and of none disdained, a capteine against whome fortune never frowned, nor mischance once spurned, whose people him so severe a justicer both loved and obeied (and so humane withall) that he left no offense unpunished, nor freendship unrewarded; a terrour to rebels, and suppressour of sedition, his virtues notable, his qualities most praiseworthie.

(*Ibid.*, p. 130)

. . . Wantonesse of life and thirst in avarice had he quite quenched in him; vertues in deed such an estate of sovereigntie, youth, and power, as verie rare, so right commendable in the highest degree. So staid of mind and countenance beside, that never jolie or triumphant for victorie, nor sad or damped for losse of misfortune. For bountifulnesse and liberalitie, no man more free, gentle, and franke, in bestowing rewards to all persons, according to their deserts: for his saieng was, that he never desired monie to keepe but to give and spend.

(*Ibid.*, p. 131)

INDEX

Authors

Bailey, John, 126
Barber, C. L., 123
Bronowski, J., 117–118, 124
Brooke, Tucker, 119

Campbell, Lily, 54

Danby, John, ix, 77
Dowling, Margaret, 66

Empson, William, 65, 71

Fergusson, Francis, 40–41

Goddard, H. C., 44–46, 75, 126, 131
Gregg, W. W., 64

Handover, P. M., 68–69
Harbage, Alfred, ix
Harrison, G. B., 120
Hart, Alfred, 5, 63
Heffner, Ray, 65–66

Jenkins, Harold, 125–126
Jorgensen, Paul, 64–65, 67–68

Kirschbaum, Leo, 63
Kuhl, Ernest, 73

McCurdy, H. G., 73
Morgann, Maurice, 119

Pafford, J. H. P., 161

Read, Conyers, 72
Ribner, Irving, 5, 71
Rossiter, Arthur, 24, 65

Smith, J. H., 64
Smith, Red, 18
Stevenson, R. L., 42
Swift, Jonathan, 50

Traversi, Derek, 45–46, 48

Wilson, John Dover, 48–49, 122, 123, 125, 126, 127

Yeats, W. B., 45

Subjects

Alexander the Great, 16

Burghey (William Cecil), 34

Cecil, Robert, 34ff
censorship, 4–5, 6, 8, 9–11, 22, 29, 36, 64, 65–66
Chamberlain's players, 22, 29, 34, 65–66
Coleridge, 24, 136

Dering MS, 69–70
Digges, Dudley, 68
Dionysus, 133
Don Quixote, 141
Drayton, 13

Essex, 21–22, 34ff, 42, 71–72, 119–120; *Apologie*, 37–38, 69

Faithful Shepherdess, 151
Famous Victories, 13, 82–83, 86, 88–89, 112, 123, 125
Fletcher, John, 143–144, 147, 157–158

Gaultree Forest, 5, 12, 33, 57, 64–65, 66, 71
"Great Chain of Being," 24, 51, 58
Gulliver, 50

Hakluyt, 121–122
Halle, Edward, 67, 121
Hayward, John, 22, 66
Holinshed, 13, 27, 33, 35, 38, 43, 56–58, 67, 70, 91, 102, 121, 122–128, 162–163
Horace, 157
horsemanship, 73–74

Iliad, 103
Irish Expedition, 21, 34–35, 38
Isle of Dogs, 29, 36

Johnson, Samuel, 128
Jonson, Ben, 36

Lyly's *Euphues*, 18–19
Lyrical Ballads, 136

Maid's Tragedy, 148, 156
Mary of Scotland, 64, 71–72
Mucedorus, 161

Nash, Thomas, 23–24

Pandosto, 154–155, 161
Philaster, 160
Plato's *Ion,* 136
Plutarch, 17
Puttenham, 147

sack, 36, 120

Shakespeare

Characters

Antigonus, 161
Aumerle (*Richard II*), 79
Bolingbroke, *passim*
Bottom, 136–137
Brutus, 3, 100
Carlisle (*Richard II*), 73
Chief Justice, 61, 86, 111ff
Cordelia, 55, 98
Exton (*Richard II*), 72
Falstaff, 16, 33, 51, 84, 86, 110ff, 127, 129
Feeble, 52, 62
Florizel, 151, 154
Fluellan, 16, 49–50
Francis, 77, 119–120
Gower, 49, 51, 73
Hermione, 145, 155–156
Hotspur, 76, 78, 86, 90, 99–100, 124, 133
John of Lancaster, 11–12, 30, 32ff, 57, 64–65, 66, 68, 102–103, 110–111, 116–117
Katherine of France, 41, 58, 59
Leontes, 145, 148
Mercutio, 61, 133–134
Monmouth (Hal), *passim*
Perdita, 145, 149–150, 152ff, 157–158
Pistol, 37–38
Poins, 60, 104–106
Polixenes, 148, 150ff, 156–157

Richard II, 64, 71–72, 88
Rumour, 25, 27, 37
Shallow, 51
Stanley (*Richard III*), 64
Theseus, 132ff, 141, 156, 160
Vernon, 85
Williams, 52–53, 56, 62

Works

As You Like It, ix, 144, 151, 155
Coriolanus, 130
Cymbeline, 144, 147
Hamlet, 40, 100–101, 105, 118, 126
Julius Caesar, 148
King Lear, ix, 55, 59, 118, 130–131, 148
Love's Labour's Lost, 137–138
Macbeth, 115, 134
Merry Wives of Windsor, 13, 15–16, 36, 58
Othello, 18, 130
Richard II, 8–10, 22, 29, 97
Romeo and Juliet, 61
Sonnets
29: 96
52: 94ff
114: 160
121: 17, 75
124: 15
125: x–xi, 10
The Tempest, 77, 118
Timon of Athens, 130
Troilus and Cressida, 43, 130

Southampton, Earl of, 34, 72

Tamburlaine, 117
Thoreau, 30

Upanishads, 118

Whitgift, 21–22, 58
Wordsworth, 18, 136